PRAISE FOR
PLANES, CANES, AND AUTOMOBILES

"The table of contents reads like a list of your biggest worries when planning a trip with an older loved one, all of which Grubb puts to rest with her intuitively written and expertly researched chapters. Grubb's travel experiences with her mother, Dorothy, have resulted in . . . a delightful guide full of important information for those of us who want to enjoy the companionship of our best travel partners, our parents."

—**Samantha Brown**, television travel host and
AARP Travel Ambassador

"In writing *Planes, Canes, and Automobiles*, Valerie Grubb has created a handy guide to managing travel planning, packing, problems, and expectations for adult children and their parents. Valerie's love and respect for her mother—and Dorothy's for her—shine through every page of this delightful, eminently useful book, a must-read for anyone planning a multigenerational vacation or a trip with older parents."

—**Nancy Parode**, senior-travel expert and writer for About.com

"My trip to Normandy, France, last year with my 85-year-old father and 91-year-old uncle was a deeply emotional journey made immensely more satisfying because we followed Grubb's insightful advice from day one. *Planes, Canes, and Automobiles* not only offers practical tips for older travelers, but also speaks to the joy of sharing a travel experience with someone you love, no matter the age difference."

—**Deb Wood**, collections manager of Stranahan
House Museum and avid traveler

"Valerie Grubb has thousands of miles of travel under her belt, both alone and with her mom. As a result, *Planes, Canes, and Automobiles* is chock full of practical and highly useful advice and information derived from personal experience. Follow the tips in this book to create your own great vacations and memories with two, three, or even four generations of family."

—**Eileen Gunn**, founder of FamiliesGoTravel.com

"As a wheelchair user for more than seven years, my family and I have personally used many of Valerie's recommendations in our travels. More importantly, I have shared her insights as educational material with new wheelchair users. When it comes to travel for those with mobility restrictions, *Planes, Canes, and Automobiles* is the best resource available."

—**John Berkey**, management consultant and co-founder of Able Challenger

"Valerie M. Grubb's *Planes, Canes, and Automobiles* is a must-read for anyone wishing to travel with their elderly parents. Written in a direct, engaging tone, Grubb addresses many of the difficulties and joys of going on the road—from dealing with your parent's reluctance to travel to detailed packing lists and clever resources you shouldn't miss to help you enjoy your vacation. *Planes, Canes, and Automobiles* is a one-stop-shop for the grown and flown wanting to take their aging parents on a vacation."

—**Lorraine C. Ladish**, author and founder of VivaFifty.com

"*Planes, Canes, and Automobiles* is a practical guide that deals with the logistics and the emotional aspects of traveling with an older family member."

—**Candy B. Harrington**, author of *Barrier-Free Travel: A Nuts and Bolts Guide for Wheelers and Slow Walkers*

PLANES, CANES, AND AUTOMOBILES

CONNECTING WITH YOUR AGING PARENTS THROUGH TRAVEL

VALERIE M. GRUBB

RIVER GROVE
BOOKS
www.rivergrovebooks.com

This publication is designed to provide accurate and authoritative information in regard to the subject matter covered. It is sold with the understanding that the publisher and author are not engaged in rendering legal, accounting, or other professional services. Nothing herein shall create an attorney-client relationship, and nothing herein shall constitute legal advice or a solicitation to offer legal advice. If legal advice or other expert assistance is required, the services of a competent professional should be sought.

Published by River Grove Books
Austin, TX
www.rivergrovebooks.com

Distributed by River Grove Books

Design and composition by Greenleaf Book Group
Cover design by Greenleaf Book Group
Cover images: ©shutterstock/vectorgirl; ©shutterstock/Macrovector
Interior images: ©Kelley School of Business at Indiana University/Josh Anderson

Publisher's Cataloging-in-Publication data is available.

Print ISBN: 978-1-966629-90-0

eBook ISBN: 978-1-62634-217-0

First Edition

For Mom, who told me that I could be anything
I wanted to be if I just put my mind to it.

I still believe you (although at this point in my life
I'm starting to doubt I really can be a ballerina . . .).

CONTENTS

ACKNOWLEDGMENTS

My deepest thanks to my editor, Marsha Jane Brofka-Berends, for providing far more than her editing prowess. The publication of *Planes, Canes, and Automobiles*, as well as my blog, *Travel with Aging Parents*, would not be possible without her insight and expertise. I look forward to working together with her on my next book!

I would also like to express my gratitude to the many others who helped make this book a reality: Tanya Hall and the entire Greenleaf Book Group team for ushering this work into print; Christine Wilson and MtoM Consulting for helping me to grow *Travel with Aging Parents* from an idea to a blog and beyond (and for sharing stories about travels with her grandmother); Brooke Smarsh for her legal advice (without which chapter 13 would not exist); Douglas Zeiger for his travel medicine expertise; and Jennifer Fitzpatrick and her husband, Sean, for their brainstorming efforts on the book title. Thanks, too, to Jeanne Kelly, Will Perry, Ruth Schick, Susan Combs, and Jeannette Franks, who generously shared their knowledge with me.

I also wish to thank my friends and the readers of *Travel with Aging Parents*, who gave me encouragement—and motivation—to write this book. I am especially grateful to everyone who completed the survey that formed the basis for chapter 13. Also thanks to Dan, as well as "Brittany," "Charles," and "Lindsey" (you know who you are!) for offering advice on how to travel with challenging parents or parents-in-law. Thank you for sharing your stories with me!

Finally, to my brother, Eric: for all our fun adventures together—both those we've already had and those yet to come.

TRAVELING WITH PARENTS

Because my dad was a corporate pilot and our whole family accompanied him on *many* trips (his bosses always welcomed his bringing us along), I was practically born in the air. Those early years of travel influenced how I spent every spare dollar and vacation day as I grew older, and I developed a passion for exploring the world with my parents, with my friends, and even on my own if no one could go with me.

Although I occasionally traveled with my parents, my "busy life" and adventures with my friends typically took priority over family outings. When my father died unexpectedly in 2005, I realized how many trips we had discussed taking as a family but never got around to doing—and that they would remain untaken. The week after Dad's funeral, Mom, my brother, and I went to Washington, D.C., because that city had always been at the top of Dad's list of places for us to visit together. It was crushing not to have him there with us, and to this day I regret not going on that trip while he was still alive.

At that moment I made up my mind to avoid the same situation with my mom. Since then, she and I have taken numerous trips together—both in the U.S. and overseas—and now travel with each other several times a year. I used to believe that my burning desire to travel came from my father, but through our adventures together I've come to realize that I get it from Mom, too! She and I love seeing new sights, meeting different people, and experiencing other cultures. By traveling together, we've found that we both embrace differences and marvel at similarities. We've figured out that a challenge encountered while traveling makes for a great story when we're back home and (most of the time) even gives us something to laugh about on the road.

If you haven't traveled with your parents in a long time (or at all), remember that they won't be here forever. Each trip with them that remains untaken is a missed opportunity for you all to connect on a more meaningful level *as adults*. Traveling together as grown-ups has a different (and in many ways better) dynamic from the family vacations of your childhood. Give it a try—I think you'll like what you find.

True, travel with aging parents can pose some challenges. But taking a vacation with your parents is very doable and can actually be enjoyable! (Yes, you *can* have fun with your parents! Who knew?) So let go of the past, embrace the future possibilities, and go create some new memories!

To your future travels,

Val

NOTE TO READERS

I've organized this book thematically, but some of the information and advice I present applies to more than one section. To avoid repetition, when a subject comes up multiple times, I've discussed it in detail once and mentioned it briefly (with cross-references to the fuller discussions) in other places.

To avoid cluttering the chapters with phone numbers, website URLs, and other reference-type data, I've put most of that stuff at the back of the book in a section called "Resources," which is organized by chapter. Nearby you'll also find some sample checklists that I hope will help you with your travel preparations, as well as some sample itineraries that I hope will inspire you and your parent to start planning your own trips together!

Finally, rather than making assumptions about whether you'll be traveling with both parents or with just one (and then making further assumptions about which parent that might be), I've decided to write as generally as possible and use both "a parent" and "parents" throughout the book. My own experiences involve travel primarily with my mom, so my personal examples mention just one parent.

UNDERSTAND THAT THINGS HAVE CHANGED

The journey of a thousand miles begins with a single step.
—Lao Tzu

In the sixth century BCE you might have been able to start a trip just by taking that first step out the door. Nowadays, though, if you want to realize your dreams of relaxation and rejuvenation, you'll need to go beyond a single step and include military-precise planning—and infinite patience. Add to the mix an aging parent who either asks to come with you or is someone you wish to bring along and the planning process becomes much more complicated, because your parent's needs and abilities will strongly influence where you go and what you do while on vacation.

Multiple surveys have proven the health impacts of taking time away from a stressful work environment. But studies indicate that retirees, too, benefit from vacations. If your first thought is "Vacation from what?" keep in mind that retirement can cause boredom, depression, disconnectedness, or a sense of life becoming "stale"—all feelings that can result from normal day-to-day routines, regardless of age or employment status.

A proper vacation, where we unplug and relax, is supposed to remove us from our normal routines so we can recharge our batteries. Clearly, anyone at any age can benefit from a good vacation. Depending on your parents' physical and mental capabilities, however, they may need extra assistance in order to travel. And that is where you as the adult child come in. Fortunately, the rewards far outweigh the challenges. Family vacations can be incredibly satisfying, because they enable multiple generations to connect (or reconnect) through unique and special travel experiences!

My First Solo Trip with Mom

When was the last time you spent two weeks on vacation with your parents? When I was younger, of course, I could count on my yearly trips with my parents to see Mickey Mouse in Florida and my grandparents in Altoona, Pennsylvania. Once I went to college, though, my choice in traveling companions changed, and I opted to travel almost exclusively with friends.

That changed in 1994. I had graduated from college with my engineering degree in 1990, and although I'd promised myself I would use my precious two weeks' annual vacation to go somewhere exotic every year, *four years* had passed without a single trip. I was "too busy" and "way too important" (aren't we all at that age?) to consider taking time away from the office for something as trivial as a vacation.

My then-supervisor at Rolls-Royce in Indianapolis brought me to my senses by informing me that no one wins prizes for turning in unused vacation time. He also pointed out that the company had survived for more than 175 years without me and would continue to survive while I was out of the office on vacation. After getting over the shock of this revelation, I decided to go for it and test his theory. Thinking "Why wait?" I booked my time out of the office for one month out and planned a trip to Italy, which had always been at the top of my list.

Unfortunately, none of my friends could get vacation time approved on such short notice. Nervous to travel by myself, I had the crazy idea to ask my mom if she was interested in going with me. I call it "crazy" because as adults none of my friends or I had ever traveled anywhere alone with a parent. In fact, the thought of doing so hadn't even crossed any of our minds!

Although since graduation and moving out on my own, I'd been more interested in establishing my independence than in traveling with either of my parents, in 1994 I was too much of a wimp to go to a foreign country by myself. My brother was long gone from the house, and my dad was a pilot whose work took him away from home much of the time. That left my mom as the only readily available traveling companion.

I was racked with anxiety at the thought of traveling with Mom. Since I had moved out on my own, we had never spent more than a weekend together. Spending 10 days together in a foreign country sounded as crazy to me as taking time off from work. At the same time, though, I wanted someone to go with me. So I bit the bullet and invited her—and she said yes.

At the time Mom (then 64) had one requirement for coming along: prebooked hotel rooms in Rome, Florence, and Venice (she was okay with figuring out everything else on the fly). Although I was originally miffed about having to book rooms ahead of time (rather than wing it—my preferred option, which Mom wasn't comfortable with), after the trip I realized that the prebooking was the best decision we had made, because during the trip I had enough adjustments to make to Mom's style (and vice versa, I'm sure!) without also having to worry about where to lay our heads each night.

During that first trip, I found out that Mom requires a minimum of an hour and 15 minutes to eat any meal (including snacks or coffee and dessert), that she cannot skip meals (something I frequently did), and that she *must* have eggs for breakfast (a meal I typically skipped). On our last morning in Venice, we got into a huge fight because after sleeping late we couldn't find a place that was still serving eggs. After we had been searching for almost an hour, Mom started crying because she was upset at me (for being mad at her) and fatigued (because I had run her hard up to that point). I remember being so angry at her inability to compromise—and at my inability to find a restaurant that served eggs.

As I leaned against a post to take some deep breaths, I noticed that the restaurant two storefronts down had a sign advertising quiche, even though they'd told me they weren't serving eggs when I asked a few minutes earlier. The server at the door was surprised and delighted to see us return to his restaurant, and in true Italian fashion he couldn't help but be charming to two women traveling by themselves.

After lunch (and a few glasses of wine), I asked the waiter if he knew that quiche was made with eggs. His surprised "No!" seemed genuine, and in fact he insisted on verifying this with the chef (and owner), who set him straight. He then sat down with us for an additional glass (or two) of wine. Although our lunch wasn't the fanciest meal we had in Italy, it was the most hard won—and one that established a baseline for our travels ever since! Twenty years later, our trip to Italy remains one of the best vacations I've ever taken. For the first time in my life I saw my mom as a person, not as a tormenter who existed solely to question my choice in both men and lipsticks. Our travels together these last two decades have increased my respect for her and strengthened the overwhelming love I have for this person who has become a friend in addition to being my parent. Mom still doesn't like my lipstick choices (though at least she's pretty much fine with any man I introduce her to now), but travel has brought us together in a way that no number of phone calls could ever equal.

Things Have Changed—and Are Still Changing

Jetting to Italy was the first long-haul trip for both Mom and me and the first one we did together. Since that first trip we've shared many adventures both inside the U.S. and in such faraway destinations as China, Cambodia, Thailand, France, England, and Australia (to name a few). In the 20+ years we've been traveling together, perhaps the greatest difference between when we started and where we are now is how much Mom's tolerance for things outside her routine has decreased (even though she says she loves to travel around the world). Yes, I've found eggs for breakfast in every location we've visited, and I always factor in plenty of time for meals without annoyance. But I've found that as she's aged, she's become less tolerant of cultural differences.

Many studies indicate that people become less adaptable to change as they get older. When you're traveling, particularly to a foreign country, the differences can be more jarring—and that can cause angst to Mom (which then ripples my way). As someone who lives alone, Mom has also gotten used to extreme quiet. So when we visited my brother and his family when they lived in China, between his twin toddler girls and toys that constantly made noise (thank you, Thomas the Tank Engine!), Mom was a bundle of nerves ready to jump out the window.

Mom's stress causes her to get angry, upset, and short with me, too. Over time, I've learned not to take this personally, though. I'm ready for it and do my best to make light of the situation to help her calm down and handle all the change going on around her. I've found this approach (and attitude) to be the difference between a disaster and a good time—and it also prevents me from going out the window myself!

In addition to the psychological factors you need to be prepared for while traveling, physical issues may also affect your vacation. If your parent is still physically active and can easily get around, you won't need to worry about this. But if your parent needs more assistance, you may have to shift away from your usual role as the child in this relationship and become the caregiver and problem solver. The effect of this change on your psyche can be not only profound but surreal—and is further compounded when a parent strongly resists this shift. (I've experienced this myself: Mom doesn't want to miss *anything* when we're on a trip, yet there are plenty of activities that I can do that are beyond her physical abilities.)

It's a careful balancing act: adopting the decision-making role while not assuming the parent role. Be careful not to treat your parents like children when planning a vacation, and especially once you're on vacation, because doing so can destroy any chance of enjoying this time together. They deserve your respect for their parenthood status, and treating them any differently (even if you're making all the decisions) is a recipe for disaster.

Your Parents' Input Matters, Even If You're the One Footing the Bill

Remember, it's your parents' vacation too, so your preferences aren't the only ones that count. And in addition to the physical and mental changes that may have occurred in your parents, there may also be financial shifts in the relationship you have with them. Chances are that when you were younger, *they* planned and paid for family vacations. That dynamic can shift once your parents retire and have fixed incomes. This is definitely something you need to be aware of when surveying the landscape for potential destinations.

Through experience, I've found that the need to modify my approaches and expectations—and the need to compromise (and maybe not get exactly what I want)—varies, depending on the makeup of my travel party. I treat my solo vacation time as an opportunity to be completely self-absorbed and do only what *I* want to do. When I travel with other people, I shift my expectations to include their input as well. And when I travel with Mom, I adjust my outlook even more—and therein lies the potential for conflict.

When I'm traveling with friends, I'm fine with them chiming in on where to eat and what to do throughout the day. Interestingly, I don't always give the same respect to Mom's input. At times, for example, I feel like she's imposing, and I think (sometimes emphatically), "We should do what *I* want to do, especially since I'm the one who's paying." Her input sometimes strikes me as an intrusion on the great vacation I've planned. Through our thousands of miles together, though, I've come to realize that there is something in the parent-child relationship that inherently creates conflict, and my mentality of "I'm an adult now and don't need my parents' input anymore" can still shape that relationship even when I'm all grown up.

When those feelings arise, I have to remind myself that vacation with Mom is *not* just about me; instead, it's something we're sharing *together* (and by the way, I need to check my attitude). I owe it to her to ensure that she's comfortable and happy when we're traveling together—and that I'm not suffocating her into submission. *Her input matters.* If it doesn't, then I shouldn't take her on vacation with me at all.

Tackling the Taboo Topic: Money

If your parent will be contributing to the vacation, it's imperative to keep his or her budget in mind as you evaluate options. If you're someone who prefers to hike your way through a country, this may be the time to leave the backpack at home, because your parent will almost certainly need more comfortable sleeping arrangements than a sleeping bag or cot (as well as hot water and breakfast). On the other hand, he or she may object to a five-star hotel on the grounds that it's too expensive (even if you've found a deal so good that the Pope couldn't pass it up).

You may need to factor into your expenses the time it takes to get to your destination as well as potential health concerns. For example, visiting such far-flung locales as China and Thailand can require plane rides in excess of 15 hours, depending on your starting point. Such long trips can increase my 84-year-old mom's risk of developing deep vein thrombosis (DVT), a blood-clot formation that's especially prevalent in the legs and increasingly likely to occur as people age and when they are immobile, as on long plane flights (see chapter 7 for tips on avoiding DVT). Having more room and the ability to prop up her feet helps Mom decrease that risk on long flights, so several years ago my brother and I decided that it was best for her to fly business class (which offers foot rests and other amenities) on long trips. Because those seats are well beyond what Mom can afford, though, he and I purchase her ticket (or use miles) to get her up front. If your parent is in similar circumstances, you may need to factor a higher priced ticket into your trip planning, depending on your parent's age and where you're going.

The geography of your destination can also affect the trip cost. The more challenging the terrain, the more critical it is to arrange for local transportation, especially if convenient and accessible public transportation isn't available. Private cars and taxis add up quickly but can mean the difference between your parent being able to participate and him or her having to sit in the hotel, waiting for your return.

Don't forget to factor hotel location into your cost, too. It may be less expensive to stay on the outskirts of town, but if you're not near the tourist sites, you may pay more in cab fares than you would pay for a hotel closer to the action. Mom and I experienced this firsthand when we went to London to see the world premiere of *Casino Royale* (we're both huge James Bond fans). We stayed at a location outside the city and saved a significant amount of money on lodging—all of which (and more!) was eaten up by cabs to get us back into the city to see the museums, plays, and other attractions. All told, we spent much more each day on cabs than we would have spent on a more expensive hotel in the city.

If finances are tight for your parents, consider covering some or all of their trip costs. For example, to help cushion the hit to Mom's budget when she and I visited my brother in China, he and I typically split the vast majority of her trip expenses. When just Mom and I travel together on our own (and we aren't visiting other family members), I put together an estimated budget, and then she and I discuss how much she has in her checking account and what she's comfortable spending. I'll typically cover the cost for both of us for anything particularly extravagant (such as some ridiculously priced restaurant that I want to try). Without this cost sharing, I'm not sure she would ever leave the house; or even if she did, once we reached our destination she might not leave her room because she finds everything "too expensive." Absorbing the costs for Mom's activities and other daily expenses (such as food) while on vacation helps lessen her financial concerns about traveling.

Planning for a vacation is also a great opportunity to start a conversation with your parents about their finances in general. This conversation can give you a sense of how your parents are doing financially and overall and how things look for the future. If you're not already involved in your parents' finances, discussing a travel adventure may be a great way to bring their financial situation out in the open and perhaps give you both peace of mind about any concerns in that area. My regular chats with Mom about her money, for example, have helped her feel a lot less anxious about it.

Many people are reluctant to have frank conversations about money. But it's important to discuss trip costs with your parents—and any financial limitations they, or you, have that could affect your trip together. Some aging parents (such as my mom) are worried about having enough to cover their retirement years, for example. This fear, and others like it, is very real to your parents. To keep everyone happy and excited about taking a trip together, be prepared to have an up-front discussion with your parents about their expected financial contribution and then adjust your travel plan accordingly or, if possible, supplement your parents' portion of the cost.

S-l-o-o-o-o-o-w Down

Like your parents, you, too, may find it difficult to accept that they may no longer be able to do everything they used to on past vacations. After all, who likes to think of our parents (and subsequently ourselves) aging? So when you are considering traveling with your parent, it's best to discuss potential trip activities *before* you start to look at locales. Understand that what they enjoyed doing in the past may not be possible for them today (whether or not they admit it).

During a recent trip to Sydney, for example, Mom wanted to explore the city's famous opera house. But the usual tour—an arduous affair involving over 200 steps—was more than she could manage. By planning well in advance of our trip, I learned about, and reserved, a limited-mobility tour of the opera house. It allowed her to achieve her goal of exploring the building even while in a wheelchair and offered an even better behind-the-scenes peek than the regular tour, since we got to take the cast and crew elevators!

Not all activities worked out so great on that trip. Mom was determined to do the 1332-step climb up the Sydney Harbour Bridge, even though she struggles with the 10 stairs in her home. She couldn't accept the fact that she would not be able to do it. (It also didn't help that some random stranger at a restaurant where we ate lunch told her to "go for it!" and not let her children tell her what to do.) Even if it had been just the two of us, I'm confident Mom could not have done it, even if we could have taken our time and moved at her pace. But the climb is done in a group of 12 people who are tethered together, so Mom's physical limitations would have affected more than just our immediate family. Alas, I had to be the bad guy and cancel her participation. She was upset with me, but I wisely bought a video that showed the whole climb so she could see there was no way she could have done it. Only then did she calm down—although I think it took her another 24 hours to stop being mad at me for being the Fun Police.

If you're not sure of your parents' activity level, I strongly suggest taking a stroll with them, even if it's around the mall, to garner firsthand knowledge of their abilities and pace—something that is as critical. Knowing this information well before you head out on vacation will give you time to recalibrate your expectations and figure out activities that work best for your parents. By thoroughly understanding your starting point, you can investigate all the possible options, thus shifting the question from "What *can't* my parents do?" to "What *can* my parents do with me comfortably and safely?" (You may find that figuring out ways to help them get around easier does the trick. For example, I've rented wheelchairs, golf carts, and private cars to help move us around as quickly and efficiently as possible.)

Recalibrating your expectations about what can be accomplished will do much to ensure that everyone enjoys the vacation. You may be able to skip through the Roman Coliseum after rolling through the Sistine Chapel and climbing the Spanish Steps, for example, but don't expect your parent to have the same energy level. In fact, a good rule of thumb is to take in one major site and then have a rest period. Breaking up physical activities with a casual meal (something that can take hours in Italy's capital and many other places) gives you a chance to talk about what you and your parent saw and to deepen your shared appreciation of the moment. And partaking in the traditional pastime in Italy—or France, or wherever—of eating ridiculously slowly and chatting up everyone will give you a new perspective on how the locals live, which is something you'd miss entirely on a typical whirlwind schedule!

The key here is to remember that on a trip your parents *might* need some extra time (and patience) to handle the increase in physical activity. Remember, though, that slowing down can benefit *you* as well. How many times have you come home even more exhausted after going full-tilt throughout a jam-packed vacation? Being more relaxed about time will help you enjoy your travels more—and experience less stress.

Don't Forget Medical Considerations

Adding more time to your vacation schedule to accommodate mobility issues is but one consideration when planning a vacation with an aging parent. Before choosing a destination, it's important to have a thorough understanding of your parent's specific medical needs, because they may play a role in your selection process. Although it may feel strange, conducting an informal "interview" with your parent will go a long way toward helping you gain a complete picture of what medical issues you'll need to consider when planning your trip. I'll discuss medical considerations in depth later in this book, but for now consider the following questions as a starting point:

- What medications are you currently taking and on what schedule? (Depending on the length of your trip, your parents may need a vacation override from their insurance carrier to make sure they have enough to cover the entire time they're away from home.)

- Do any of your medications need to be refrigerated or require other special handling? (This is of particular concern on long-haul flights, where you'll need to arrange for onboard refrigeration.)

- Do you require daily shots? If so, do you administer the shots yourself, or will you need assistance? (If your parent needs assistance, you'll need to identify an on-site location with a health-care provider, such as a nurse or doctor, to administer the medication.)

- Do you have any airborne allergies? (The severity of your parent's allergies and time of year when you're traveling could be factors when selecting locations.)

- Do you have any other special medical considerations (pacemaker, need for dialysis, etc.) that I should be aware of?

Once you have a clear picture of your parent's medical needs, it's important to understand your role while you're on vacation together. Although he or she may never miss a pill while at home, a break in routine makes it harder to remember these schedules—almost certainly resulting in confusion and frustration for your parent. This problem is particularly exacerbated when crossing time zones: the greater the time change, the harder it is for your parent to get back on schedule (at least without your assistance). Of course, some people handle changes to routines well; but for many people, breaking schedules—even for fun activities—can be catastrophic to their medical regimes. Later in this book I'll discuss additional medical preparations, such as getting vaccines, traveling with oxygen, handling prescriptions, and many more topics. For now, know that it's critical to be aware of your parent's medical issues in order to ensure that he or she stays healthy while on vacation.

If You're Already Exhausted . . .

If the thought of all this preparation is exhausting you already, might I suggest hiring out? There are some great all-inclusive options out there (see chapter 9). Giving a travel professional your specifications and letting him or her offer up suggestions may be the ticket to the happiest and most relaxing vacation you've ever taken!

Another option is to select a vacation destination within easy driving distance of your house and book hotels that allow changes to the reservation. That way, if you wake up on departure day and either you or your parent isn't prepared to go anywhere, you can postpone your plans by a day in hopes that tomorrow will be better. This flexibility can also help reduce any anxiety about losing money if you need to make last-minute changes to your plans. A nearby location also lets you and your parent try a short weekend getaway before committing to a longer period of time together.

And don't forget cruises! They may seem cliché, but there are some fantastic cruise options out there now. Gone are the days of one or two cruise lines. Now big ships abound—and they're fighting for your business. Several cruise lines cater to the physical needs of an older crowd while also offering full amenities and activities for younger generations. Many lines can arrange transportation from where you live to the ship without your having to think about a thing. This is especially helpful if your parent lives in a different city from you. The cruise line can even get you and your parent to the ship at approximately the same time so you can walk on together—something that is important to my mother.

You Can Do This!

Bette Davis once said (though my mom insists this is her own original saying), "Growing old is not for sissies." Remember, growing older isn't easy for your parents—my mom is *not* happy that she can't do all the things she wants to do. But keep in mind that you don't know how long you'll have to enjoy your parents' company. So take advantage of every moment—including bringing them along for vacations. No experience in the world expands your horizons and offers the potential for amazing shared experiences as much as traveling with your parents, which can be an incredibly fulfilling experience if you approach it with the right frame of mind. As our parents age, their new frailties can sometimes reshape our relationships with them. In our childhoods, it was our parents who made all the decisions and took *us* along. Now those roles are reversed, and it's *our* turn to step up and plan the trips. As you start the planning process, know that *you can do this*!

PICKING A DESTINATION THAT WORKS FOR EVERYONE

Travel and change of place impart new vigor to the mind.
—Seneca

In travel, as in real estate, it's hard to overstate the importance of "location, location, location." *Where* you go sets the tone for your time away from home or the office. If you're up for adventure, for example, a locale off the beaten path can let you push yourself to your limits physically. If learning is your thing, a Road Scholar program to someplace new can help you expand your knowledge of archaeology, geology, history, or numerous other fields. Feeling altruistic? Volunteer programs throughout the world offer opportunities to work with the less fortunate or assist with scientific research, for example. Or maybe you want a break from the daily grind in your everyday surroundings—and in that case, a change of scenery might be all you need for a great vacation.

Those are all outstanding reasons to head out on vacation—and there are many more besides those! But to achieve your travel goals—whatever they may be—you first need to spend some time figuring out *where* to go. And that means investigating various locations to ensure that the destination you choose meets your and your parents' needs. That's the sort of decision I rarely take lightly when I travel with a small group of friends, and it's one I'm even more careful about when I travel with an aging parent.

Unless I'm traveling solo, though, I have to remember that the location decision isn't just up to me. Whenever you have traveling companions, you have fellow decision makers. If you're traveling with your family, for example, I'm guessing you wouldn't dream of booking a destination without consulting your spouse (and maybe even your kids, too). It's no different when it comes to traveling with aging parents: their input matters—*even if you're the one paying for the vacation.* Depending on your parents' physical abilities, selecting a locale may require a bit of work in order to ensure that they can safely enjoy their vacation, so getting their opinions early on can help you all narrow down the location options. Asking for their input has a major side benefit, too: involving your parents in the location-selection process can set the perfect "together we'll tackle the world" tone for your upcoming adventure!

I recommend that both you and your parent compile separate lists of places you want to see. Then compare them, identifying similarities (in specific destination or theme), and target your top two or three locations. If your parent is confined to a wheelchair and wants to hike Mount Everest . . . well, that may be a problem. (Although a Sherpa guide could probably be arranged to carry Mom or Dad up the mountain for the right price!) Most of the time, however, your parent will pick a location that, with proper planning, can be navigated by even the most physically challenged.

If your parent is reluctant to make suggestions, focus on what you're both trying to get out of the vacation—relaxation, adventure, opportunities to try new food, etc.—in order to build excitement about the destination options you've identified. Starting the vacation planning on such an upbeat note can put you all in the right frame of mind to get through the rest of the trip planning (which can sometimes be a challenging process). Keep in mind that this trip might be a major event that your parent looks forward to—and something that revives his or her drive or motivation. After all, who among us hasn't lost a little steam after going through the same routine for months on end? Aging or retired parents experience that too. Humans are creatures of habit, and we can find ourselves weighed down with stale routines at any point in our lives.

Some compromise may be necessary when selecting locations and sites to visit. On my own, I can power through three Italian cities in a week—but that pace becomes more challenging to maintain if I'm pushing Mom in a wheelchair. After years of traveling with her, I've realized that I see *more* when I slow down. So now I spend more time in one place instead of cramming in as many cities as I can. Whether Mom and I are in a large city or a tiny little town, we get to know a place better by taking the time to explore the full range of activities there—and sometimes we find unexpected surprises. During our travels Mom and I have taken cooking classes, for example, and gone on tours that included stops in local residents' homes. (When we decide to sign up for tours, we target those that offer more in-depth information, a slower pace, and exposure to the local culture.) These experiences make a trip so much more relaxing and enjoyable. And as someone who likes a good meal paired with a delicious wine, I've found it isn't so bad to take extended breaks to stop and smell the roses (or drink the *vin*) every now and then!

If your parent is nervous about taking a big trip or has a health condition that makes travel logistically challenging, consider doing a "test run" first—a mini-trip to a nearby location (see chapter 9 for suggestions). Visiting a new area in close proximity to your parent's home may be just the ticket to get everyone excited and motivated for an extended vacation to a "bucket list" destination!

Before Selecting a Location

It's critical to discuss potential trip activities during the early stages of travel planning, because your parents' preferences and abilities may have changed over time, as yours probably have, too. Don't assume that what they've done for the past several years still interests them today. So to avoid spending a lot of time researching options that won't work, be sure to find out first what they can and want to do on vacation.

When reviewing potential locations, keep in mind the purpose of the trip. Do you and your parents want to relax and read books, for example? Are any of you the type of traveler who likes to explore new places and cultures? Do you want your vacation to include both relaxation and activity?

In addition to questions about activities and preferences, also consider questions about your parents' health and abilities, such as the following:

1. Do your parents have any preexisting conditions (such as heart or lung disease, or blood disorders such as anemia) that would make air travel difficult? If so, consult with their doctor before finalizing a location that requires a long-haul flight.

2. Is the location you're considering currently under any health warnings? Check out the Centers for Disease Control travel health notices to determine if any alerts have been issued for certain areas. Such alerts will probably affect your choice of destination, because older individuals belong to a high-risk population that's more vulnerable to many diseases.

3. How mobile are your parents? Can they navigate a city where walking is the typical mode of transportation (e.g., Rome or New York City)? If your parent cannot walk or has difficulty doing so, it's critical to know how navigable a destination is via wheelchair. I also recommend finding out the availability of local taxis or car services that can be hired hourly or daily, because this type of transportation is a great way to reach sights that are beyond walking distance from your hotel. (And car service won't necessarily break the bank: in many Asian countries, hiring a driver for the day is incredibly cheap and can easily be factored into your budget.)

4. If your parent needs medical attention while on vacation, what is the availability of first-class hospitals or doctors at your destination? When Mom seriously injured her knee while hiking through the

jungles of Cambodia, the only readily available health-care practitioner we could find was a local witch doctor (seriously). Although I've been hurt while traveling, that experience wasn't nearly as traumatic to me as seeing my mother in pain and feeling a lack of confidence in the medical care she was receiving. As Mom has continued to age, we've made sure to pick destinations (and hotels) with ready access (preferably on-site) to top-notch medical care. We also check for hours of operation and find out the exact location of the medical care. "Accessible" doesn't necessarily mean "on-site and available 24 hours a day."

5. Are your parents overly sensitive to heat, sun, or cold weather? If you're looking at a beach vacation, keep in mind that walking in sand can be difficult for an aging parent, particularly one who walks with a cane. To help overcome this challenge, look for a location with beach wheelchairs, which have knobby tires that don't sink in the sand, so your parents can participate in the fun. Cold locations have their problems, too, such as ice. In those places you'll need to be extra careful (and take your time!) to ensure that your parents don't slip, fall, and get hurt—or even break something.

6. Do your parents have continence issues? If so, they'll need quick access to bathrooms, a requirement that may mean avoiding travel to less developed countries—such as India or Vietnam, for example—or planning for frequent stops during long-distance car travel—such as a cross-country road trip.

7. Do your parents have allergies or other health issues (such as asthma) that could be affected by the air at the location you select? For example, several cities in China are ranked among the 10 most smog-filled cities in the world. I've been to China many times, and even though I'm pretty healthy and don't have asthma, I've sometimes had issues breathing there. If your parent has chronic obstructive pulmonary disease (COPD) or uses oxygen, the local air quality can significantly affect your choice of destination.

8. Do your parents get carsick on bumpy, winding roads? And can your parents drive if necessary? (When Mom and I went to Hawaii, I got so carsick on the twisty road to Hana that she had to take over the driving!)

9. What dietary restrictions or preferences do your parents have that might play a role in selecting a vacation destination? Because my mother has severe colon issues, for example, we make sure she has access to non-spicy, bland foods wherever we go (or else we have serious problems down the line). If you or your parents like to cook a leisurely meal on your own, renting an apartment with kitchen facilities may suit you better than staying in a hotel.

10. Finally, what activities do your parents like? Water aerobics? Hiking? Lounging on beaches? Selecting a destination with activities that your parent enjoys doing will help everyone have a great time. Multiple options also let you and your parents go on separate adventures and do some exploring on your own.

This long list may seem daunting, but don't let it deter you from taking a vacation with your parents! Traveling with an aging parent can be one of the most rewarding activities of your life—for *both* of you. As long as you do a bit more planning before selecting a destination, everyone—including you—will enjoy the trip!

Traveling with a Wheelchair-Bound Parent

When planning any trip, I always consider affordability and whether the location has lots of great attractions. But because Mom has difficulty getting around and often uses a wheelchair, we also have to look for a few other key features in our vacation destinations: ample barrier-free transportation, ADA-compliant hotels, and close proximity (and easy access) to the things we want to see and do. Over the years, the most important thing I've learned about most travel destinations is that if you do your research and plan ahead, it's possible to have a great vacation that includes lots of fun activities *and* meets the needs of wheelchair users.

When looking to rent a wheelchair, start by asking your hotel to arrange to have one available for your exclusive use. If the hotel already has a wheelchair, it's probably reserved for transporting guests to their rooms and therefore isn't available for one guest to use off the hotel property. In that case, the hotel may (with enough notice) be able to obtain another wheelchair you can use exclusively during your stay.

If the hotel does not offer this service, find out if wheelchair rentals are available at your destination by searching online for the name of the location and "wheelchair rentals." In the U.S. alone, for example, you'll find options in many regions, including Care Medical Equipment (Orlando, FL) and Wheelers Mobility (Arizona). Many destinations have tourism boards that can answer questions on this subject; you can find their contact information by doing Internet searches for a location name and "tourism board."

You can also consider taking an electric wheelchair with you—either your own or one you've rented before leaving home. One terrific option, a foldable power wheelchair, is much lighter and smaller than its nonfoldable counterpart, making it easier to transport. If you decide to take any type of electric wheelchair with you when you travel, though, first check out Mobility International USA's website for important information and tips on voltage converters, plug adapters, and travel insurance coverage for these devices.

You never know what useful information you'll stumble upon through Internet keyword searches. When I was researching wheelchair rentals in Sweden for an upcoming trip, for example, I came across a website called ForHandicapTravelers.com that rents amphibious wheelchairs to help people with mobility issues enjoy the waters of the Mexican Caribbean! (So now, if Mom and I decide to take a beach vacation one winter, I already know of at least one place with some great amenities for her!) But you'll never find such surprises—or even the information you intentionally set out to find—unless you take the time to look.

Some destinations are difficult to navigate with any kind of wheelchair—for example, places with steep inclines, narrow streets, or cobblestones. But if you really want to visit one of those places, look into alternative modes of transportation, such as hiring a private car, before crossing it off your list. With a little extra planning, the mobility challenged can access many travel destinations, so don't let a wheelchair stop you or your parents from seeing the world and checking places off your bucket lists!

Overcoming a Parent's Reluctance to Travel

I've mentioned the importance of seeking your parents' input when considering vacation locations (see chapter 1). This helps them feel that they're part of the process, starts to build their excitement for the trip, and enables you to find out if there is someplace they would like to visit. But what happens if your parents are reluctant to travel? What if you ask them to go with you and they won't commit to the trip and instead prefer to stay at home?

Even after all the traveling Mom and I have done together, she *still* gets anxious and hesitant when I start discussing our next trip. Through the years (and thousands of miles), I've figured out some good tactics for getting her to commit to a vacation. Most of them involve examining the situation from her perspective, trying to understand *why* she's reluctant, and doing what I can to put her specific concerns to rest.

For example, if your parents are hesitant to travel with you, consider the possibility that they won't commit to a vacation because they're feeling overwhelmed by the prospect of figuring out travel arrangements and other details of vacation planning. This is definitely true for my mom: she doesn't have Internet access, so she has no idea how to even book a flight these days! So I've found that offering to handle most (or even all) of the planning goes a long way toward making her feel more at ease about a trip.

Anxiety about change is another factor that can make aging parents reluctant to travel. Change—even good change, such as vacation—is stressful for anyone. But for aging parents, the stress level can be even higher: studies show that as we get older, our tolerance for change decreases.

How you phrase your inquiry can help decrease (or increase!) your parents' stress level about travel. I used to ask Mom, "Where would you like to go?" One day it finally dawned on me that this question made her anxious, because she felt that the vacation, and my enjoyment of it, was on her shoulders. I noticed that she hesitated to give me answers and then would revisit them repeatedly, saying that she wasn't sure about her choice and we could go anywhere *I* wanted to go. The fact that she kept bringing up the subject and making excuses for her choices indicated to me that Mom felt anxious about how I'd respond to her suggestions.

So I've adopted a different approach. I now tell Mom, "I'm starting to make plans for vacation, and I'm mulling over potential locations. I'm going to do all the planning, so you don't need to worry about anything. But if there's someplace you want to explore or any particular activities (relaxing, sightseeing, etc.) you want to do, let me know, and I'll take that into consideration. Otherwise, I'm planning a vacation for this particular week. So mark your calendar, because I really want you to go!" I'm asking the same "Where would you like to go?" question, but giving her (and me) plenty of opportunities to offer input or even to opt out.

If you have a particular location in mind and are not open to destination suggestions, I recommend a different approach. In these cases, I merely mention to Mom that I'm planning a vacation for a certain time frame to a particular location and would very much like her to come with me. I also tell her that I'll do all the planning, including making her flight arrangements. All she has to do is pack her bags, and then we'll be off on another adventure together!

Doing what you can to make the trip preparation easier for your parents is another way to help them feel less anxious about travel. Mom's memory is slowly fading, so when we start discussing our next vacation I remind her that I'll send her a copy of my packing checklist to help her get ready for the trip. (By offering to share a tool that I'm using too, I'm not calling out her inability to pack on her own.) I find that if Mom thinks she needs to do anything beyond packing, she goes on a downward spiral of feeling overwhelmed (a not-uncommon experience among aging parents); at the same time, however, she doesn't want to be treated like a child and told what to do. It's a delicate balancing act between minimizing her responsibilities and keeping things as simple as possible for her so she doesn't get stressed out. By telling her that I'll take care of the big stuff, I make it difficult for her to say no to a trip together.

One final option (albeit a risky one) to consider: purchase the ticket and tell your parent when the two of you are traveling! Before you take this course of action, though, check with the airline to determine if travel insurance will allow you to modify your dates (or cancel your trip altogether) if your parent is unable to go. If you have enough frequent flyer miles, using them to purchase tickets may give you some flexibility: these tickets can typically be modified or canceled and the miles redeposited into your account easily (though the airline may have penalties for this—you know airlines and their fees!).

Sometimes people just need a little nudge to wake up their inner travel bug. So before merely accepting your parents' reluctance to travel with you, ask yourself if there is anything you can do to assure them that they'll have a great time. If you can help them overcome their hesitation and recognize that this vacation will be well worth any hassle or stress they may experience, you'll be all set for a fabulous trip together!

Lodging Considerations

Before I finalize the decision of which city or country to visit with my octogenarian mom, and particularly before booking anything that's nonrefundable, I always take a quick peek at local lodging options to make sure that she will be able to get around them on her own. This is a particularly important consideration for our trip planning, because Mom's mobility has decreased in recent years (during our last couple of trips together, she's had to rely on a wheelchair for any long-distance travel). To help with these mobility challenges, I try to find accommodations with layouts and facilities that minimize the number of stairs she has to negotiate.

The great news? Hotels can be helpful in meeting the special requirements of aging parents with physical challenges! Although I've struggled
a bit with this in some places—for example, in less developed countries,
such as Cambodia, or in smaller cities throughout Australia, to name a few
places—most hotels will do their best to accommodate their guests' needs if
you ask them for help and give them plenty of notice.

Keep in mind that a hotel's size can influence its ability to meet your
needs. Small boutique hotels may not have the full range of services that
a larger hotel has (see below), but I've found that they can typically locate
Mom and me on the first floor (to avoid stairs) or near an elevator (to avoid
long walks down a hallway).

Large full-service chain hotels (Marriott, Hilton, Westin, etc.) will
ensure that their operators are in compliance with the Americans with
Disabilities Act (ADA), a U.S. federal law that, in part, requires hotels
to provide full access to people with disabilities. Some independent
operators, however, may either be unaware of the law or fail to meet
its requirements. This is especially likely in foreign countries, where
the ADA is not the law of the land and accessibility regulations vary
widely, if they exist at all. In addition to being ADA-compliant, large
chain hotels usually have more resources to meet special needs. These
resources can include shower chairs, rooms with handrails, lightweight
door knockers, large-button phones, TTY or TTD phones, and other special equipment. A 2010 update to the ADA requires hotels and other
businesses to meet certain accessibility requirements in any swimming
pools they have. Among other things, they must now provide a fixed pool
lift or sloped entry to assist guests with entering and exiting the water.

When it comes to making arrangements with a hotel, the traveler's primary responsibility is to take ownership of the process. *Be specific.* Know
exactly what you need—and communicate those details to the hotel. For
example, if you call the hotel and ask a vague question such as "Do you have
ADA-compliant rooms and equipment?" the agent will almost certainly
say yes. But when you arrive, you may find that the hotel's ADA-compliant

items do not meet your particular needs. So instead of asking general questions, specify which accommodations you need. For example:

- "We require a room next to the elevator."
- "We need a roll-in shower, a bathtub with handrails, or a chair in the shower."
- "We require sheet guards on the bed." (Not all hotels stock these regularly, but full-service hotels should be able to provide them.)

Again, understanding your parents' needs and giving the hotel as much detail as possible *before* you book will ensure that you can arrive at your destination confident that their needs will be met.

An Alternative Lodging Option: Cruising

If you're considering a cruise, or any other water-based outing, first discuss with your parents whether they get seasick. You'll also want to determine what type of medical care is available on the ship, in case your parents do become ill. Although ocean and river cruising offer many great features (especially in terms of activities for both you and your parents), medical care on ships can be sketchy. So be sure to research them in advance.

As you evaluate potential trip locations, find out if cruise lines visit any of them. If a cruise line does indeed stop at a city you're considering, you may find that paying a short visit to that place as part of a broader itinerary appeals more to you and your parents than staying put in one place for your entire vacation. One appeal of cruising with an aging parent (particularly if he or she has mobility issues) is that your lodging moves from place to place. No more unpacking, packing, and moving from hotel to hotel—just let the ship do all the work!

A cruise ship also allows you to explore several destinations or relax onboard, poolside. If you've never taken a cruise before, you may be surprised to learn what modern cruising is like. Cruise ships vary tremendously in size, amenities, and activities. Some of the so-called megaships (such as those from Norwegian Cruise Lines and Royal Caribbean, for example) can carry *more than 4,000* passengers, whereas smaller ships (such as those from Paul Gaugin Cruises) might carry only 300 passengers. As a general rule, the megaships have more activities (including zip lines, rock climbing, and Vegas-style live shows, for example) and are less expensive than small ships, which tend to focus more on community- or learning-based activities. On larger ships, you're also more likely to encounter more families; smaller ships, on the other hand, often attract an older clientele with more disposable income. When considering any cruise, regardless of size, be sure to read the fine print to find out which activities are included in the price and which carry additional fees.

Final Thoughts

The key to enjoying a vacation with an aging parent (or anyone, really) is to relax and take it slow. How many times have you gone on an action-packed vacation only to return home as exhausted—or more so—than when you left? (I've often experienced this myself!) And of course there's the need to slow things down a bit—or even a lot—when traveling with an aging parent.

Remember, if you want your aging parent to have fun on your vacation together, then *you* have to have fun yourself. So figure out what works best for the two of you and what helps you make the most of each other's company.

THE ART AND SCIENCE OF EFFICIENT PACKING

I have learnt that I am incapable of packing the
right amount of clothing, probably because I start
10 minutes before I'm supposed to leave.
—Marcus Brigstocke

Packing can be a bear, particularly if you're trying to help your parents with this task and they live far from you. If it's not done carefully, you run the risk of forgetting something critical, resulting in vacation hours wasted in search of suitable alternatives. I experienced this firsthand a few years ago during a trip to Spain, when my mom forgot to pack shirts. Instead of exploring the sights, we spent hours shopping (an activity we both dislike) to find clothes for her. I made a mental note right then to add to my pre-vacation checklist the action item "help Mom pack." Fortunately, careful preparation can make packing a breeze—even if your parents live in a different state.

Before getting into the specifics of *how* to pack, let's first review *what* to pack. As you go through this chapter, begin compiling a packing list that can be shared with your parent to help him or her get ready. I tailor my packing list to our specific destination and typically share it with Mom a month in advance of our trip. This gives her enough time to pick and choose among her existing clothes and purchase any items she doesn't already have or needs to replace. Using a packing list is a good way to ensure that neither of us forgets something critical—and that we don't wind up spending valuable relaxation time in a department store!

Prescriptions and Other Medications

This is perhaps the most critical category on your packing list. Many seniors require certain medications or specialized equipment, and some of these items can be difficult (if not impossible) to obtain in another country. So be sure your parent has enough of these supplies to last for the entire trip, as well as extra medication in case of delayed or diverted flights that extend your vacation. I usually carry an extra week's supply of medications, which is enough to handle an emergency and to get Mom settled back at home following the trip. Even if the vacation is not particularly strenuous, the travel portion can be tough on her, and not having to deal with getting refills on her first day back ensures that she doesn't miss a pill.

Your parent should bring all medications (both over-the-counter ones and prescriptions) in a carry-on bag so they'll be available if they're needed in transit. Keeping them in a carry-on also ensures that a lost or delayed piece of checked baggage won't interrupt your parent's medication schedule. Also make sure all medications—especially prescriptions, but this applies to over-the-counter items as well—are not in a pillbox but in their original packaging with the label on the outside. I learned this lesson the hard way when Mom and I were stopped in Chinese customs and not allowed into the country until I returned more than 200 pills to their respective prescription bottles and provided a doctor's note detailing the prescriptions. (Fortunately, I've always carried such a note when traveling outside of the U.S. since a friend had this issue while trying to enter China.) Being locked in a 6'×6' room with a guard—and without our passports—was *quite* stressful! There is already enough tension when you're going through security checkpoints on a *good* day, let alone when you encounter problems because the customs officials can't identify your parent's pills!

As a standard practice when traveling with an aging parent, always carry hard-copy versions of these documents:

- Prescription refill forms for all of your parent's doctor-prescribed medications. If requested by security or customs staff, they can serve as verification for the medications your parent is carrying. They're also important to have in case your parent needs to refill a prescription or has a medical emergency during your trip.

- An updated list of all of your parent's prescription and nonprescription medications. Be sure to include each drug's generic name in case you need to get a refill during your trip. Drugs have different brand names in different countries, and knowing the generic name will enable you to get what you need faster. (If you want to find Tylenol overseas, for example, you'll need to ask for it by its internationally recognized generic names, paracetamol or acetaminophen.)

- Contact information for all of your parent's doctors.

It's also a great idea to have electronic versions of these forms (as well as scanned copies of your passports) parked at an e-mail account that you can access from anywhere in the world, in case the paper copies are lost.

In addition to prescriptions, New York City–based travel medicine specialist Dr. Douglas Zeiger recommends bringing over-the-counter items to help with any heartburn, diarrhea, or stomach issues that might arise due to changes to your parent's diet or schedule. He also offers these suggestions:

> You should bring with you any over-the-counter medications that you take on a regular basis, such as acetaminophen or ibuprofen.

Bring diphenhydramine (antihistamine) for allergies and a top-ical ointment for insect bites, and if you have a life-threatening allergy don't forget a supply of epinephrine autoinjectors. Make sure, though, that your medications are permitted in your desti-nation country: diphenhydramine is illegal in Zambia, for exam-ple, and in most countries epinephrine autoinjectors require prescription documentation from a doctor.[1]

This is great advice that I follow whenever I travel. After all, no one wants to arrive in another country and have his or her critical life-saving medications taken away.

When figuring out which of Mom's or Dad's medical needs require spe-cial attention as part of your trip preparation, it's best to play it safe: if you're unsure how vital a piece of information or a certain medication is, put it on the list anyway. Prescriptions and other medical supplies aren't always easy to replace when traveling internationally. So do your best to be com-prehensive. This is one situation when overplanning is a good thing. And after you've handled the prescriptions and medications, the hardest part of packing is finished!

Finally, the Transportation Security Administration (TSA) has specific rules about how to pack liquids, gels, and aerosols. In your carry-on bag, you're allowed only *one* quart-size clear plastic zip-top bag of containers with those items—*and* each container may hold only a maximum of 3.4 ounces. However, if you have liquid medications that you must carry on the plane, they don't need to go in the zip-top bag, and their containers may exceed 3.4 ounces. Such medications do need to be in their original packaging, though, with their exterior labels still intact. Pack them in an

---

1   For more of my interview with Douglas Zeiger, see the two posts titled "Dr. Zeiger, Travel Medicine Specialist" on my blog, *Travel with Aging Parents*. Part 1 is at travelwith agingparents.com/interview-part-1-dr-zeiger-travel-medicine-specialist/; part 2 is at travelwithagingparents.com/interview-part-2-dr-zeiger-travel-medicine-specialist/.

easily accessible spot: at the security screening, you'll need to place them in their own bin to go through the X-ray machine. As you go through security, keep handy a printed list of medications (both prescription and over-the-counter), prescription forms, and doctor contact information in case any questions arise, and before sending them through the machine alert the TSA screeners if you have medicines in quantities greater than 3.4 ounces. (See chapter 5 for more information about traveling with medically required liquids.)

Traveling with Oxygen on an Airplane

Although it takes a bit more planning, traveling with a parent who requires oxygen can be accomplished. Effective May 2009, the U.S. Department of Transportation (DOT) requires all U.S. air carriers to allow passengers to bring DOT-approved portable oxygen concentrators (POCs) on board aircraft. Foreign carriers must also permit POCs, but only on flights departing from or returning to U.S. soil. Even with this rule in effect, however, if your parent requires oxygen, *do not* show up at the airport and expect to bring a POC onto the plane that same day, because each airline has its own policy for onboard oxygen transport, which can include limiting the number of oxygen-requiring passengers on the same plane. Therefore, before you book any flight, it's critical to contact the airline to verify that your parent can be accommodated and to determine the airline's specific requirements.

Rules for airlines outside the U.S. (i.e., for travel not originating from or returning to the U.S.) are less consistent regarding allowances for passengers traveling with oxygen. Thus in these cases it's even more important to check with the airline prior to booking a flight and to get in writing any of the airline's agreements and requirements.

The *only* approved oxygen device allowed onboard flights is a portable oxygen concentrator, which is a smaller, lighter, and easier-to-carry version of a home oxygen concentrator. No other personal oxygen systems are permitted, and filled oxygen tanks (containing either liquid or compressed gas) can *never* be brought on board—or even checked as baggage—on *any* airline. Some airlines may allow empty oxygen equipment to be stowed in the baggage hold, but it must be verified as empty, and the regulator must be removed. Ask your airline ahead of time if it allows empty tanks to be checked.

An airline's website may list approved POCs. Two other U.S.-based organizations also list approved devices (and include lots of other helpful information about air travel with supplemental oxygen): the Airline Oxygen Council of America and the National Home Oxygen Patients Association (see resources list in appendix 1).

If your parent's oxygen provider cannot provide you with a POC approved for air travel, you'll need to rent or purchase one. The organizations above and the airlines can usually give recommendations. If you're traveling with an approved POC, that status will need to be indicated on the POC itself. Whether a POC counts toward your two-item limit for carry-ons varies from airline to airline, so be sure to check your airline's particular policy. Knowing how much carry-on space you have to work with is especially important if you need to bring with you other medical supplies, snacks, or entertainment options.

Most (if not all) airlines require a written physician's statement indicating that your parent requires oxygen and is "fit for travel," and that his or her medical condition would not necessitate "extraordinary medical assistance" during a flight. Your airline may require you to submit a specific form or request a statement on your doctor's letterhead, so check on this rather than assume that a note from the doctor will suffice. Most airlines require this documentation two weeks or so before a flight, so don't wait until the last minute to ask about their policies.

You'll also need an official prescription form (which must be carried on your person through security and on the flight) indicating that oxygen is required and possibly a separate medical information form as well. If your airline requires any documentation from your doctor, be sure to get confirmation (preferably in writing) from the airline that it was received. This should help you avoid any issues at the airport. Just in case, though, when boarding your flight bring extra copies of all paperwork with you.

The FAA requires a POC to have 150% of the flight time in battery life, regardless of how long the user may choose to use the device. (For example, if your flying time is three hours, you will need four and a half hours of battery power.) The appropriate number of batteries can be calculated based on the manufacturer's estimate of the battery life while the device is in use and on information provided in the physician's statement (e.g., flow rate for the POC). An airline carrier may deny boarding to a passenger who does not carry enough properly packed batteries to accommodate 150% of the flight time. If you find the thought of following this policy a bit overwhelming, I recommend renting a POC from a provider familiar with your airline's requirements and letting them deal with all the details.

Planning for and undertaking any trip already involves some amount of anxiety—and when one of the travelers depends on supplemental oxygen, the anxiety level has the potential to go way up. But it doesn't have to be that way! With a little extra research and planning, traveling with supplemental oxygen can be a piece of cake.

Shoes and Clothing

Once the medical-related items are squared away, the rest of packing is a relative breeze. Right behind medications (and underwear!) is what I consider the second most important item to pack when traveling with an aging parent: appropriate footwear. My mom does *not* like exercise and therefore does little of it when not on vacation, so when we travel she walks much more than she's used to (even though I arrange wheelchairs whenever and wherever we go). So on our trips I want to make sure she brings the shoes she needs to handle the increase in activity. As she's packing, I go through her footwear options in detail over the phone and help her select one pair of dress shoes (for evenings), one pair of casual sandals, and one pair of walking shoes (to wear on the plane). Because she almost never gets rid of shoes (even long after any support is gone!), I often send her new walking shoes to take on our trips. That way I know she has at least one great shoe option that's extra cushy and comfortable. And getting a new pair of shoes helps build her excitement for our next trip.

The items your parent needs depend on the type of trip you're taking, of course. Many experienced travelers offer this hard-earned advice: "Lay out on your bed all the clothes you think you'll need for your upcoming trip. Then put half of them back in the closet." Other great advice includes separating your clothes into three piles:

1. Clothes you *must* have with you on the trip
2. Clothes you *think* you might need on the trip
3. Clothes you could make do without

Once you've separated your clothes into these three piles, push yourself (or your parent) hard to leave behind items in the second and third groups. If something isn't absolutely necessary, leave it at home! After all, that's one fewer item you'll have to tote around. Leaving a bit of empty space in your suitcase also means you'll have room for a purchase or two when you're on vacation. And with today's airline baggage fees, minimizing the amount of luggage you bring can save you a lot of money, too.

When I travel, for my daytime outfits I typically plan on getting two to three days' wear out of every bottom (slacks, skirts, shorts, jeans, etc.), and one day—perhaps two, if I don't spill anything on it—of wear out of each top. So for a seven-day trip, I'll bring three bottoms and six tops. I also bring items that I can mix and match into different outfits. (For example, I rarely bring a blouse that can be worn with only one particular pair of pants.) As for evening wear, I also bring either two tops and one bottom, or two dresses. Even though Mom and I usually prefer to eat at casual local establishments, it's good to be prepared in case we decide to do something fancy.

When on vacation, neither Mom nor I worry about ironing: we're both fine if a shirt or dress comes out of the suitcase with a few wrinkles. After all, we're *on vacation*! That said, because I'm determined both not to iron and not to look like I've been sleeping in my clothes, I avoid bringing linen or other clothing that seriously wrinkles. Materials with the best track record for emerging wrinkle-free from a suitcase include the following:

- Cotton knits and cotton-knit blends (unless treated, pure cotton typically needs ironing, while knit blends still look good after being folded and packed for hours on end)
- Wool and cashmere
- Anything made of 100% nylon or polyester knits
- Most sweaters
- Denims (though lighter denim pieces, such as skirts, may need a quick once-over with an iron)

In addition to the basics, you and your parent may want to bring items specific to your destination and your planned activities there. If you're going on a walking tour in the mountains of Nepal, for example, you'll need sturdy boots. Planning to lounge on a Hawaiian beach? Don't forget your sun hat! And if you're planning an evening at the Paris Opera, you'll need formal attire. Chances are, though, that you and your parent will be spending most of your time simply exploring, and for those days casual, everyday dress is all you'll likely need. Be sure, though, to research what constitutes acceptable "everyday" dress at your destination, because some cultures frown on certain fashions—such as shorts or sleeveless tops, for example.

Packing Toiletries

If you'll be sharing a room with your parent, it's worth the time to compare your parent's toiletries with yours so you can avoid bringing duplicates. (What a waste of space and weight, for example, if you both bring shampoo!) As part of our trip preparations, I send Mom a list of the items that I'm bringing (well, at least those that I'm willing to share with her), in case she wants to use mine rather than pack her own. I also discuss the following recommendations with her to help ensure that all of our toiletries make it to our destination safe and sound:

- Don't bring full-size bottles of shampoo, conditioner, gel, etc. Instead, conserve space by putting what you'll need for the trip in small, travel-size plastic bottles. Although it may not seem like much, the weight of your containers adds up. So saving even a few ounces here and there can make a difference.

- An airplane's cargo hold isn't pressurized, so don't fill your bottles completely. A too-full bottle may explode if its contents don't have enough room to expand. There is nothing worse than arriving at your destination after a long plane flight only to discover that half your clothes need to be sent to the hotel cleaner because face moisturizer (or, worse, Pepto Bismol!) oozed all over everything.

- If you've ever watched baggage handlers at work, you know that they do a lot of tossing and throwing of bags—including anything marked "fragile"! Therefore I pack *all* toiletries (not just liquids) in plastic zip-top bags that can contain spills if a container does break. I group similar items: all face products in one bag, all hair products in another bag, etc. This organization helps Mom and me easily find the items we need after arriving at our destination.

- I pack all of my smaller toiletries and makeup items in one large, clear vinyl travel bag. It organizes my things, lets me quickly find what I'm looking for, and prevents hairbrush bristles from snagging my clothing.

Packing Jewelry

Mom and I usually leave our jewelry at home when we travel. But if we're planning to attend a fancy event (such as the performance at the Sydney

Opera House that we attended a few years ago in Australia), we'll bring a few special items and hand-carry them with us on the plane. Whether you're bringing everyday jewelry or fancy stuff, these tips and tricks might help you transport them more easily and securely:

- Keep earrings organized in a multi-compartment pill case. Another option is to use a safety pin to poke holes through an index card, then fit your earring posts through the holes.

- To keep jewelry pieces from rubbing against each other and therefore getting damaged, pack them in separate zip-top bags. (Snack-size and sandwich-size bags are the most useful sizes for this.)

- To keep a delicate chain from tangling or breaking, open the clasp, snake one half of the chain through a drinking straw cut almost to half the length of the chain, then reclose the clasp.

- Store everything in a travel bag specifically designed for jewelry. This type of bag typically has multiple pockets and storage compartments, often has padding for extra protection, and can be rolled up for easy packing.

Packing Breakables

I typically try to avoid bringing fragile items with me when traveling, because baggage handlers are so brutal with luggage and I try to keep my carry-ons to a minimum. However, every now and then when I'm on vacation I find something that I feel I cannot live without. And then I have to figure out how to get it home in one piece.

In my luggage, I usually pack a few WineSkins (a brand of resealable, bubble-wrap-lined plastic sleeves). They're small when not in use, so having them with me "just in case" doesn't inconvenience me. And when I find a wine that warrants the effort, I'm prepared to pack it. So far I've had fabulous luck transporting bottles in these bags on direct flights, though I've never taken the risk on a connecting flight—that would involve too much handling (and more opportunities for breakage) in my book. In checked luggage, the TSA has no restrictions on wine or spirits with less than 24% alcohol content, but prohibits anything with more than 70% alcohol content; each person may have up to five liters of alcohol between 20% and 70% alcohol content. (Be sure to check if your home state has its own restrictions.) When returning to the U.S., you can purchase wine or spirits in duty-free shops overseas and bring them on board with you, but if your international flight ends in a U.S. airport that isn't your final destination, you won't be able to take that alcohol into the cabin for your next flight and will either have to dump (or drink!) it or put it in your checked luggage. The rules around transporting alcohol can be tricky, so be sure to check them carefully at the U.S. Customs and Border Protection website.

To transport any delicate gifts or tchotchkes (including those wine bottles), I first encase them in bubble wrap. Then I center the bundles in my luggage and surround them with my clothes. I usually cram my dirty clothes into a hotel laundry bag, and I've found that the middle of that bag is also a great place to pack breakables.

Additional Items to Pack

Careful planning regarding hard-to-replace and critical items ensures that Mom and I don't forget anything that's vital when we go on a trip. Our packing lists include plenty of "ordinary" things, too. None of them is a matter of life or death, but I still consider them must-haves for any traveling parent:

- A light sweater and a jacket. Layers are the key to feeling comfortable in a wide range of temperatures, but because Mom is often cold, having additional clothing available is a must. Light layers can be tied around a waist or stuffed into a bag when not in use.

- If your parent wears glasses, an extra pair. Like keys, glasses are the sort of thing for which spares are always a good idea. (Bring paper and electronic copies of the glasses prescription, too, just in case.)

- If your parent uses a hearing aid, bring lots of extra batteries.

- A magnifying glass and a pen light for reading the small print on maps, bus schedules, menus, and tourist brochures.

- Toothpaste or denture cream, as well as a travel toothbrush. There's nothing like waking up on a plane and brushing your teeth (or dentures) to refresh your mouth before landing!

- A day-trip bag for excursions. This could be a backpack, a messenger-style bag, a tote bag, or even a small purse—whatever your parent needs to keep essentials (such as medicines) close at hand during outings.

- A small umbrella that fits easily into your parent's day-trip bag. It's also a good idea to carry an extra plastic bag or two with this, so that a wet umbrella can be easily stowed when the sun comes back out.

- Snacks, water, and entertainment (e.g., reading material, playing cards, media players) for the journey. These items go in the carry-on bag, and although they aren't quite as essential as medicines, they are pretty valuable for making a long plane ride more enjoyable. Because liquids in amounts over 3.4 ounces aren't permitted through security (see earlier in this chapter), either plan to purchase water at an airport shop, or bring an empty bottle and fill it up for free at a water fountain near the boarding gate.

Cramming It All In

Now that you've narrowed down what you're going to pack, it's time to get it all into your suitcase. Flight attendants, pilots, and other travel experts usually recommend rolling clothes instead of folding them, because rolled items take up less space and have fewer wrinkles. I follow this great advice myself, but even when Mom sees my stuff come out of the suitcase looking fine, she still wants nothing to do with rolling her clothes. So instead of pushing this packing plan with her, I focus on helping her choose clothes that can all fit into her suitcase when folded.

If your parent is more flexible than my mom when it comes to packing, encourage him or her to give rolling a try! Roll soft items (such as underwear, jeans, most everyday dresses, sweaters, cotton pants, and other knitwear) tightly and place them on the bottom of your suitcase. Then fold clothes made of stiffer fabrics (such as cotton shirts, jackets, and dressy clothes) and place them on top of your rolled items, staggering the waistbands so the thickest parts of your clothes aren't stacked on top of each other; doing this will save a significant amount of room! Placing dry-cleaning bags between your folded clothes and on top of the whole stack can help them move around enough (but not too much) to keep wrinkles from setting in. Don't let *any* empty space go to waste! Stuff your shoes with toiletries, eyeglasses, or other small items (even chargers for your electronics), then fit them along the sides of your bag. Place jewelry and any remaining toiletries in the center of your bag and surround them with clothes to help protect them in transit.

Before we put a single item in our suitcases, though, Mom and I identify which clothes we'll need when we reach our destination. As we pack, we make sure to lay those items on top of everything else. So if Mom and I are fighting jet lag upon arrival, we don't have to fight our suitcases, too! We can easily find fresh clothes to wear right away, without having to unpack and repack everything (which can be particularly annoying when we're moving on to a different city in fairly short order).

Remember the rule of thumb for packing clothes, toiletries, and anything else for any trip: *keep it simple*! Also remember that you (and possibly your parent) will have to carry, pull, or lift your luggage at least part of the time, so don't make the mistake of packing more than you can handle—or, more likely, more than you'll use. If possible, put everything in a wheeled bag with an extendable handle, a type of suitcase that's easiest for Mom or Dad to transport on the trip. If your parent needs a second bag, choose a small one that fits neatly on top of the bigger suitcase.

Don't forget to take precautions (for both your bag and your parent's bag) against misplaced, mistaken, or stolen luggage. For example, tie a ribbon, handkerchief, or bright tag onto your bag's handle to help you readily identify it in the baggage claim area—and to help ensure that other people don't confuse your bag for theirs. Be sure to label the inside of your suitcase with your name, your cell phone number (or that of another family member traveling with you), the telephone number of your hotel, and your e-mail address. (For security reasons, don't include your home address. You can give it directly to the airline staff if your bag is delayed and they need to deliver it to you later.) Also, take a picture of your luggage to help you describe it to the airline if, while you're in transit, it decides to take a separate vacation from you. Such a photo proved an invaluable aid during my last trip to China, when my luggage was lost and the person helping me did not speak English. If I hadn't had a picture of it with me, I'm not sure *what* we would have done!

Ready, Set, Go!

The information presented here is a jumping-off point for you and your parent to develop your own packing lists. You'll need to figure out the specifics of your own plan based on Mom's or Dad's medical needs, your destination, your transportation, and the activities you're planning for your trip. To get started, consider asking your parent to start writing a packing list on a piece of paper, then review it together periodically in the months and weeks leading up to your trip. If your parent is tech savvy, you could work on the lists together via a shared online document or spreadsheet.

Sometimes these sorts of trip preparations can feel overwhelming, so be ready to step in and lend your parent a hand if he or she needs help. Arranging directly with your parent's doctors and caregivers to get lists of emergency contacts, prescriptions, and other pertinent information can take one task off Mom's or Dad's plate (although keep in mind that your parent will need to sign a release allowing the doctor's office to give you this information). If you don't live near your parent and he or she needs someone to help with packing, consider enlisting the help of a local home-care aide.

Working together, you and your parent can figure out what items you need to bring on your trip—and what items you can leave at home. Careful planning will make the trip go smoothly so you can both enjoy your time together.

STAYING HEALTHY WHILE
ON THE ROAD

The greatest wealth is health.
—Virgil

Getting sick is always the pits, but it's even worse when you're on vacation. In addition to wasting money and precious vacation time, an illness on the road can be even more difficult to manage when you lack ready access to the prescriptions and over-the-counter medications that can help you get better faster. Adding insult to injury, getting sick while traveling can be worse than usual, simply because you're not home: there's a lot to be said about the benefits of being in your own bed when you're unwell! Unfortunately, travel can often make us more susceptible to illness. In addition to the risk factors present at your destination, conditions during the journey itself can increase your odds of getting sick. (Who among us hasn't felt the first hint of a sore throat—or something even worse—after sitting on a plane for hours surrounded by coughing passengers?) Doing what you can to ensure that you're as healthy as possible *before* embarking on vacation is a good precaution for you to take—and doubly so for your aging parents. In addition to being healthy before you go, your pre-trip preparations should also include knowing how to stay healthy while you're on the road.

The oft-quoted phrase "knowledge is power" holds true when it comes to taking your parents' medical situation into account when traveling. But children often aren't aware of their parents' prescriptions, let alone the changes that have occurred in their parents both physically and mentally over the years. Not knowing this information before you go off on vacation together can add to your stress level and—depending on your parents' medical needs—can even have serious consequences. So before you hit the "buy" button on flights for a trip with your parents, have a conversation with them about their current abilities and medications.

On my blog, *Travel with Aging Parents*, guest author Christine Wilson wrote about how a trip with her 91-year-old grandmother made her understand how important it is to be fully aware of—and to be prepared to handle—the medical issues of aging travel companions:

> In the summer of 2010 I made the 12-hour drive with my 1-year-old son and my 91-year-old-grandma to her home on Cape Cod. After my grandfather's death, my grandmother moved to an assisted living facility in Virginia, and I had not been to visit her in quite some time. I did very little to prepare for the trip except for packing Ronan's diapers and clothes for the two of us. Within two hours after starting our trip north, however, I realized that I was completely unprepared for the angst that overcame my grandmother. She was anxious about getting out of the car at the rest stop and got confused about how to use the restroom facilities. Then she refused to eat lunch and became extremely anxious again when it was time to get back in the car.
>
> Unfortunately, this was just the start of what proved to be the longest summer I've ever had on Cape Cod (and not in a good way). Looking back, I see the many mistakes I made on this trip with my aging grandma. The rest of the family knew that

she forgot things occasionally, but my grandpa had covered for her so well that we had no idea she was actually suffering from undiagnosed Alzheimer's.[2]

Assessing Your Parent's Current Situation

I won't kid you: this is a hard topic to bring up and one that everyone may be reluctant to discuss (even more so than money!). As Christine Wilson's story highlights, however, ascertaining the medical condition of your aging parent or grandparent *before* you pile into the car or jump on a plane is critical to ensure that everyone has a good time—Grandma included. Although diagnosing the onset of dementia or Alzheimer's requires medical training, you *can* try to ascertain whether your parents have any medical issues that may affect their ability to go on vacation with you and enjoy their travels, especially with such a drastic change to their daily routines.

The ideal way to gather this sort of information is through firsthand observations and face-to-face conversations. If you and your parents live in different cities, however, you may want to make a special trip to visit them for just this purpose. If that's not an option, send your parents information about where you're going together, then follow up with questions about the itinerary to gauge their feelings and understanding about the trip. *Pay attention to the answers.* If your parent doesn't remember that you're going on vacation, that's an indication of serious medical issues that may require you to take him or her to a doctor instead of on a trip. If your parent cannot discuss basic details of current events widely covered in the news, that could also be a warning sign of possible medical problems.

Another indication that your parent should see a doctor is if he or she seems to be withdrawing socially and is no longer doing favorite activities or seeing friends. Again, only a doctor can diagnose a more serious medical condition. But anyone can and should do a rudimentary assessment (even

---

2 See Christine Wilson's post, "Traveling with Grandma," on my blog, *Travel with Aging Parents* (travelwithagingparents.com/traveling-grandma-guest-post/).

over the phone) of a parent's health before planning a trip together, in case there are signs of any conditions that warrant a visit to the doctor.

If it's general anxiety that you're hearing over the phone when you mention going somewhere new, don't panic: this isn't an uncommon response. Even after all the traveling Mom and I have done together (300,000+ miles and counting!), she *still* gets anxious and hesitant when I start discussing our next vacation together. Your goal is to assuage your parents' fears and get them excited—rather than worried—about the trip. Your parents might reveal their anxiety by peppering you with lots of questions or making negative comments about the trip location or the vacation in general. This anxiety likely results from them feeling overwhelmed about figuring how to get there and the other details of vacation planning.

For example, in airports my mom is always terrified that she's going to miss her flight or be unable to find her gate. How the latter would ever be possible in an airport as small as the one in her hometown of Indianapolis is beyond me. But it's not about what *I* think—it's about what *Mom* thinks. Her fear is therefore very real and very valid. And it's something I need to handle.

To alleviate Mom's anxiety about dealing with airports, whenever I can I start our trips together by meeting her in Indianapolis so we can be on the exact same flights—even if our connections take us back to New York City, where I live. If I'm not able to meet her in Indianapolis, I make sure to book us on flights that arrive at our rendezvous airport as close to the same time as possible so she won't be in the airport by herself for long. And if I'm not flying all the way back to Indianapolis with her, I always depart after she does to ensure that she makes her flight.

I also arrange for Mom to have a wheelchair in each airport. Not only does this help keep her calm in those noisy environments, but it also helps her manage the big distances between some gates. Without the wheelchair, she ends up exhausted from trying to walk through the airport and anxious that she's late even before her plane leaves the ground, which is not a good way to start a vacation!

If you're not sure what your parents' physical capabilities are, ask them about any of their regular activities and about their social events with friends. A decrease in their participation level could mean that they aren't as active as they used to be—and that you'll need to slow down while in transit and adjust your activities at your destination. Sometimes a more direct approach works best: ask your parents how many stairs they climb in a day (or how many they think they can climb). Explain that you want to gauge their interest in and ability to do the activities you're considering for your vacation together. Assessing a parent's physical abilities doesn't have to be a secret when the goal is to make sure that everyone has a good time while on vacation. The key is not to ask only simple yes-or-no questions (such as "Are you able to walk?") but to ask many open-ended questions (such as "How do you feel after standing on your feet in a museum for an hour?") that will give you a real picture of what your parents can and can't do.

In addition to understanding your parents' physical capabilities, you also need to know what medications they take, as well as their dosages and frequency. To find out all this information, simply say, "I'm doing a few pre-trip preparations and putting together a list of all the medications we're taking so we have this information handy if an emergency happens while we're on vacation. Can you grab your prescription bottles and read off the labels to me?" This approach indicates that you're not singling out your parents but instead gathering this information as part of planned precautions for the entire family. Be sure to ask for any dates on the labels, too, because they will tell you if your parents are current on their medications. In addition to the dosages, don't forget to list each drug's generic name and purpose; if you lose the medications during your trip, this information will make the replacement process a lot easier.

One of the biggest challenges Mom and I face when traveling abroad is keeping her on schedule with her pills as we deal with time changes. Crossing time zones is confusing for anyone, and any changes to her schedule guarantee that Mom will forget to take her pills. *This will happen to your parent as well!* It's inevitable. So before you embark on your trip, know that it may be up to you to keep your parent's medication schedule on track.

Before I set foot on any plane with Mom, I calculate—based not on the local time but on the number of hours that have passed since the last dose—when she should take her pills while en route, and then I program the dosage times as alarms on my phone. I've also found it helpful to fill Mom's pill organizer with the medications she'll need while in transit. This shows her what pills she must take throughout the journey, and I can tell at a glance if she's on schedule or not. (Note: set aside only the pills needed for the time you're in transit, and keep the rest in their original bottles to make the customs check at your destination go more smoothly. This isn't always required, but why risk the consequences of getting an overly zealous customs agent?) Between the alarms and the pill organizer, Mom and I do well at keeping her on track with her medications—even on trips to destinations halfway around the globe, such as China and Australia.

Keeping your parents on schedule with their medications will go a long way toward ensuring that they stay healthy on the road. During the transit phase of your vacation, plenty of things can go wrong and distract you from remembering your parents' pill schedules. So do your homework before the trip by preprogramming alarms, putting reminders in a book, marking your calendar, making use of a pill organizer, or doing whatever else you must to ensure that your parents stay on schedule. Figuring it out and coming up with a plan in advance will make your vacation go much more smoothly.

Pre-Trip Doctor Visits

In chapter 2, I discussed several health considerations that should be reviewed prior to making your final decision on a destination. This analysis won't necessarily preclude your parent from going overseas or vacationing in a remote location. But it may mean that you need to consult health experts who can tell you the risks of going to a particular destination and what you and your parent need to do to protect yourselves from local health risks there. If you have any question about your parent's mental or physical capacity to safely go on a trip with you, your best option is to make a pre-trip visit home for your own firsthand assessment, and then accompany your parent to his or her doctor for advice on precautions to take based on your parent's medical condition and your vacation destination. (This is the perfect time to have your parent sign a medical release form that allows the doctor's office to discuss his or her medical situation with you.)

Keep in mind that fully preparing for a trip to a foreign country may require visits to two different types of doctors, your parent's primary care physician (PCP) as well as a travel doctor. Why two? A PCP and a travel doctor serve two different purposes for the traveler. The former typically offers suggestions, based on your overall physical health, that may affect the location or duration of your travels or the activities you undertake there. When traveling with an aging parent, it's an especially good idea to get a doctor's sign-off that your parent is physically capable of making the trip and to identify any medical issues that you, as your parent's travel companion, should be on the lookout for. Of course, this doctor visit may be unnecessary if your parent is healthy. But if your parent has any health issues of concern (such as my mom's 13-pill-a-day regimen, for example), being informed about and involved with his or her medical care is a good idea.

A visit to a travel medicine specialist (also known as a travel doctor) is another critical pre-trip preparation, because most PCPs lack detailed knowledge about specific regions outside the U.S. A travel doctor, on the other hand, can tell you what factors in another country may affect your existing medical conditions, explain how to avoid becoming sick there, and provide medicines that could prove useful if you do pick up an illness abroad. The typical PCP is not as well versed in these areas, although there are, of course, exceptions. Note that seeing a travel doctor is critical for *anyone*—not just an aging parent—planning a trip to a less developed part of the world where certain diseases not typically found in the U.S. are prevalent and your resistance to them likely nonexistent. In addition, most people who visit a travel doctor are less likely to come down with diseases for which they've been vaccinated. Travelers who understand the risks in certain areas and know how to avoid them are also less likely to get sick from illnesses—such as traveler's diarrhea—borne by insects and infected food and water. Although having this knowledge doesn't always guarantee that you'll avoid illness (as I can attest when I came back from French

Polynesia with dengue fever contracted through a mosquito bite), it *does* improve your odds.

If you're traveling to a more developed country (say, France or England), you don't necessarily need to visit a travel doctor, because, as Douglas Zeiger, a New York City–based travel doctor I've interviewed at length for my *Travel with Aging Parents* blog, points out, "Even though the risks with such travel are a little greater than staying home, they are not that much higher." He adds:

> One caveat, though, is that travel doctors specialize in vaccinations—many of which you should have, whether or not you're leaving the country. A PCP is familiar with childhood vaccination schedules but doesn't always think of vaccines for adults. For example, a travel doctor would know that anyone living in the U.S. should get vaccines for tetanus, pneumonia, and shingles, but a PCP might not be aware of that recommendation. Because a travel doctor would be on top of this, thanks to his or her deep knowledge of vaccines, seeing one makes you much more likely to get the vaccines you need even if you never leave the country.[3]

As you can see, it can't hurt to visit a travel doctor—and it's quite possible that you'll benefit from the experience. If you decide to visit a travel medicine specialist, be prepared to discuss your medical history, current medications (including both prescriptions and over-the-counter drugs), past illnesses and diseases, and drug allergies. The doctor will also need to know your exact itinerary in order to provide you with accurate information (and, if necessary, vaccines) based on your destinations.

---

3   For more of my interview with Douglas Zeiger, see the two posts titled "Dr. Zeiger, Travel Medicine Specialist" on my blog, *Travel with Aging Parents*. Part 1 is at travelwithagingparents.com/interview-part-1-dr-zeiger-travel-medicine-specialist/; part 2 is at travelwithagingparents.com/interview-part-2-dr-zeiger-travel-medicine-specialist/.

Aside from vaccinations, a travel doctor can also provide medications for ailments and diseases (such as diarrhea and malaria) found at your destination, and can advise you on which medications you are allowed to bring into certain countries.

Even though it's possible to do the research for travel vaccines on your own, either by conducting Internet searches or by browsing the Centers for Disease Control website, if you're traveling with an aging parent, I still suggest consulting a professional on this topic. Accurate vaccine recommendations can be difficult to find online, and the stakes are higher for older adults, whose immune systems are typically not as robust. So don't take any chances.

Finally, if you decide to see a travel doctor as part of your pre-trip preparations, be sure to do so about two months prior to your departure date. Not only do vaccines take time to build up in your system, but some of them must be administered in a series of injections over days or even weeks.

Losing Your Medications While on Vacation

Losing any belongings during a trip is stressful—and losing medication is especially scary. If this happens to you, the first and easiest thing to do is to contact your doctor and ask him or her to call in a new prescription to a pharmacy at your destination. This should be easy if you're traveling domestically; in fact, many domestic pharmacies have locations across the country, so you may be able to find a local branch of your pharmacy and order a refill there.

When you're traveling internationally, it's wise for you and your parent to bring an emergency prescription form from each of your doctors so you can get more medicine in the event your supply disappears. Request a letter that documents the medication you're taking as well as the medical condition that requires it. Make sure both the letter and the prescription include the medication's generic name (not brand name) so it can be recognized in other parts of the world. I suggest making digital scans of those forms, too, and keeping them in a secure place online (perhaps a web-based e-mail account that you can access from anywhere in the world) in case something happens to your hard copies.

If your medication is lost or stolen, take your emergency prescription form to a local pharmacy. (You might have to visit a few pharmacies to find one that will fill your prescription.) If for some reason you don't have this form and can't come up with another copy of it, ask a local pharmacist to call your doctor and get over-the-phone approval for a new prescription. If that doesn't work, you may need to visit a local doctor or hospital and request a new prescription. U.S. consulates in-country typically maintain lists of physicians and hospitals, including those doctors who speak English. To avoid having to find this information during an emergency, bring with you the contact information (especially the address and phone number) for the nearest U.S. consulate or embassy in each area you'll be visiting.

Neither Social Security nor Medicare provides coverage outside the U.S.—and your health insurance provider might not, either—so you or your parent may end up paying full price for any prescriptions you need filled during your trip. Before leaving home, ask your insurance company if you're covered overseas; if you aren't, look into purchasing a short-term policy that offers international coverage.

Fortunately, I haven't had to deal with losing medication, because Mom and I are hyper-vigilant about keeping it in our carry-on luggage during transit and locking it up with our passports in the room safe at the hotel. I hope you, too, never have to deal with losing medication during a trip. But if you do find yourself in that situation, it will be easier to handle (and resolve) if you've planned for that possibility *before* leaving home.

Travel Medical Insurance

Because Mom's Medicare and her secondary insurance are both severely limited in a foreign country, each time we travel I wrestle with the question of whether I should buy travel medical insurance for her, particularly since she reached her late 70s. (This isn't a concern just for your aging parents, though: even if you're a healthy young adult, it's important to check that your own existing insurance covers you outside the country.) Individuals with Medicare can receive coverage for medical care abroad in only a few highly specific situations, and usually only for Medicare-covered services:

- If a medical emergency occurs during travel within the U.S. and the nearest hospital is in a foreign country.

- If a medical emergency occurs during travel that takes a direct route through Canada to get to or from Alaska, and a Canadian hospital is closer than a U.S. one. (So if your parent needs emergency care while sightseeing in Canada and not traveling directly from one U.S. state to another, expect a fight from Medicare.)

- If a medical emergency occurs on a cruise ship either at a U.S. port or within six hours of a U.S. port.

- If the individual requires emergency (not regularly scheduled) dialysis in a hospital.

Before going on vacation, check out the U.S. government's official Medicare site, where you'll find more information on what Medicare will—or more than likely *won't*—cover. (Just remember that foreign hospitals are not required to file Medicare claims, so you are responsible for submitting an itemized bill to Medicare for reimbursement upon your return.) If your parent has a Medicare supplement plan (Medigap), he or she may be in luck: many Medigap plans offer additional health-care coverage for travel outside the U.S., so be sure to check the coverage and limitations of your parent's plan.

According to Susan Combs, president of Combs & Company, a full-service insurance brokerage firm based in New York City, an individual with medical insurance in his home country is covered on an *emergency* (a.k.a. "sudden or serious") basis only if he is outside an area where his carrier has a network. For example, if your mom has medical insurance, she would typically be covered anywhere in the world for a heart attack or serious injuries sustained in a car accident, but not if she came down with bronchitis and needed to see a doctor. Travel medical insurance, on the other hand, can encompass many more medical situations than just emergency care. "If you have travel medical insurance," Combs explained when I interviewed her, "many carriers have negotiated contracts with doctors, hospitals, and pharmacies outside of your home region or will reimburse your out-of-pocket expenses."[4]

When reviewing insurance options, ask about a package that includes evacuation coverage, which includes transportation back to a hospital in a more developed area if your parent falls ill or is injured while traveling in an undeveloped region. Although evacuation insurance usually covers remote areas, it tends to exclude war zones or politically unstable regions. So before signing up for a policy, make sure it includes your destination.

If your parent is prone to getting sick or is advanced in years, you may also want to purchase trip cancellation insurance in case illness forces you and your parent to cancel your trip. Coverage levels vary from policy to policy, but this type of insurance usually makes purchasers eligible for reimbursement of trip deposits and other prepaid fees in the event they have to cancel. My brother and I found ourselves wishing we'd purchased this type of insurance the day before our planned trip to Disney World in Florida, when Mom got really ill and wound up in the hospital. Because we didn't have trip insurance, we lost all the money we had spent up front on airfare and tickets to the park. With travel insurance, we could have recouped some of our money and lessened the financial hit of what turned out to be a nonvacation.

Some people mistakenly believe that their homeowners policies include travel insurance. Although most homeowners policies (and even some renters policies) do have some sort of travel insurance, it generally covers only items in transit (e.g., lost or stolen luggage, or in some cases a limited amount of stolen cash), but not medical costs. Insurance

---

4   For more of this interview, see the post "Travel Medical Insurance: Yea or Nay?" on my blog, *Travel with Aging Parents* (travelwithagingparents.com/travel-medical-insurance-yea-nay/).

protection offered through credit cards operates similarly: most reimburse for baggage loss and sometimes trip cancellation but don't cover medical costs or emergency evacuation.

Finally, a quick word on how much travel medical insurance costs: in short, the price varies a great deal. Influencing factors include the traveler's age, whether he or she has preexisting medical conditions, the length of the trip, deductibles, maximum coverage limits, and types of coverage. If you're planning a trip with an elderly parent, I highly recommend investigating all the different types of travel insurance. (A useful starting point is a travel insurance aggregator site such as Insure My Trip.) If Dad is frail or if you're concerned about Mom's health, definitely take a close look at travel medical insurance in particular. Fortunately, you don't have to rush any of those decisions: most providers allow purchase of travel insurance up to 24 hours before a trip begins. So you have plenty of time to do your homework and find the option that works best for you and your parent.

If You Become Ill While on Vacation

As you evaluate locations (see chapter 2), don't forget to look into the availability of first-class hospitals or doctors in each area. If the need for medical attention arises during your trip, you'll want to find care for your parents as quickly as possible. (Of course, you *always* want your parents to be healthy. But when you're on vacation, you also want them to get better so you can both get back to enjoying yourselves!) The doctors in your destination country will probably be knowledgeable about local illnesses and diseases and will know how to treat you. There is, of course, a tiny chance that you could pick up something that completely baffles the local medical community. Then again, you *do* sign up for certain risks when you choose to travel to remote regions of the world. Although that's something to consider along with your parent's present health when planning a vacation, it doesn't necessarily mean you have to rule out most destinations right from the beginning. Under the right circumstances—and with the right preparations—almost any trip is possible.

THE COUNTDOWN TO "GO!"

A good plan is like a road map: it shows the final
destination and usually the best way to get there.
—H. Stanley Judd

If you've ever traveled, you know that the days leading up to a vacation can be an extremely stressful time of balancing between planning for the trip while also preparing to be away from home and the office. (Heck, even a one- or two-day trip often requires intense preparation these days!) If you're a travel veteran, waiting until the last minute to prepare for a trip might not faze you at all. Regardless of your travel savvy and experience, though, if you're bringing along an aging parent, you'll have to figure out a lot more than the usual details before jetting off to a city on the other side of the planet—or even driving to the town next door.

A Pre-Trip Schedule
Early Planning Stages

- If you decide to use a travel provider (e.g., a traditional travel agent or tour operator) rather than book everything directly yourself, be sure to check the company's rating with the Better Business Bureau (BBB) and give your business only to well-rated companies. Get all trip details in writing from the travel provider, and double-check your transportation and lodging reservations yourself with your hotels, airlines, and other providers. Pay with a credit card so you can seek reimbursement from your credit card company if anything goes wrong. And if you sign up for travel insurance, verify with the insurer that your policy will reimburse you if the travel provider goes out of business or does not deliver the services you originally purchased.

- If you're using a tour operator in North America, verify that the company belongs to one of the main organizations that vet travel companies: the United States Tour Operators Association (USTOA), the National Tour Association (NTA), or the American Society of Travel Agents (ASTA). (Don't take the tour operator's word for it. Check directly with the organizations listed above to confirm that the provider has a current membership.) Get the company's physical business address and a non-800 telephone number, and beware of businesses that don't make their contact information easily available. Look for reviews online by doing a search for the name of the company with the word "review" and by checking review-based sites such as TripAdvisor and Virtualtourist. (Note that a lack of reviews can be as much cause for concern as bad reviews!) You can also ask for references, but I generally don't give those much weight because it's hard to verify if they're from independent clients who've used the service or if they're from company employees or the owner's relatives.

- If you haven't seen your parents in a while, now would be a good time to pay them a visit. Then you can see firsthand how they're getting around so you can factor their mobility and overall health into the destination selection and trip planning. A visit may also be a great time for you to go with your parents to their doctors for professional input on these issues as well.

- When booking flights, request wheelchair assistance on your parent's ticket to help him or her get around the airport. A wheelchair—and assistance pushing it—can be a lifesaver for both of you. (For more details on wheelchair assistance, see the section "One Week Prior to Departure" in this chapter.)

Two Months Prior to Departure

- Even if you and your parent are traveling to a more developed country, it's important to see a travel doctor to ensure that your vaccines (childhood vaccines as well as those recommended for travel to certain areas, such as yellow fever or hepatitis B) are up to date. Don't think you can wait until a week or two before departure to get your needed vaccines, though: some vaccines require multiple shots and up to eight weeks in your system to be fully effective. Keep in mind that as people age, their immune systems weaken, so keeping shots up to date is especially critical for your aging parents. Also check with your travel doctor that your prescriptions and over-the-counter medicines are legal in your destination country. (See chapter 4 for more information about travel medicine.)

- If you're someone who likes to wing it and find accommodations when you arrive in a new place, I recommend saving that style of travel for when you're on your own and not with an aging parent who's likely to prefer (and need) lodging arranged well in advance. (Because Mom typically needs to rest after any sort of activity—even if I'm pushing her in the wheelchair—I always have our rooms figured out ahead of time so there's no delay in starting much-needed downtime.) If your parent has any special needs, you should definitely make reservations several months in advance, because hotels, cruise ships, and other lodgings typically have a limited number of accessible rooms—and they can fill up quickly!

- At booking, confirm that the accommodations have the features your parents need (such as a bathroom with handrails or shower chairs, large-button phones, rooms close to the elevator, sheet guards, etc.). Hotels typically have wheelchairs to assist guests with moving between the lobby and their rooms, but if you'll need exclusive, all-day use of a wheelchair for sightseeing during your stay, be sure to discuss that with the hotel at time of booking. Follow up whatever arrangements you make with an e-mail to the hotel's general manager; get his or her name, and send a letter specifically to that individual requesting written confirmation of the hotel's ability to meet your requirements.

- Don't forget to take mobility issues into consideration when making cruise arrangements, too, particularly on the super-large ships. Request a room near the elevators, for example, so your parent doesn't have to walk too far. Many of the accessibility options found in hotels are available on cruise ships as well, so be sure to ask for them.

- If your parent requires a service dog, contact the U.S. embassy or consulate at your destination to determine if dogs can be brought into that country and what accompanying documentation (such as proof of vaccines) is needed. Note that some countries require that vaccines be administered only by certain veterinarians and at least 30 days before the animal enters the country, so don't wait until the last minute to check these regulations. Also be sure to find out the country's quarantine policy for service dogs. Australia, for example, requires all incoming dogs to spend a minimum of 10 days in an approved quarantine facility upon arrival; a service dog, however, can spend the quarantine period in the owner's home.

- Finally, to build your parents' excitement about the impending vacation, send them brochures or articles about your trip destination and the weather forecast there for your vacation period, too. This information will help them to start figuring out what clothes to bring, including any new purchases they may need to make.

One Month Prior to Departure

- Now is the time to familiarize yourself with your parents' medical regimens so you can ensure that they'll have everything they need during the trip. Keeping your parents on track with their medications will be one of the most important tasks on your plate while you're traveling together. Conduct a thorough inventory of your parents' prescriptions and over-the-counter medications to make sure they have enough medicine and other health-care items (e.g., incontinence supplies, blood glucose monitors) they need for the duration of the trip as well as a bit extra to cover any flight delays and a few post-vacation days. (To confirm that Mom has enough pills for a trip, for example, I have her count how many pills she has on hand for each prescription and tell me the exact numbers. If I tell her up front the quantity she'll need for the trip, she's likely to reply, "I've got enough" without doing an accurate count. We've been burned before when Mom ran out of pills while we were traveling overseas, so now I play it extra safe.)

- You may need to request an override to get early refills for any prescriptions (for medicines or for equipment such as diabetes supplies) that will be up for renewal during your vacation. The doctor must confirm the override with the insurance company, which in turn confirms it with the pharmacy. This process can take some time—it has taken as long as three weeks to arrange these for Mom—so don't wait until the last minute to take care of these. Make sure that the prescription override will provide your parent with enough medication for the duration of the trip plus delays and a few post-return days.

- While you're talking with the doctor about overrides, be sure to ask him or her about other medical paperwork. Get copies of your parent's prescriptions; customs and security officials both in the U.S. and abroad may request to see those papers. If your parent requires a portable oxygen concentrator (POC) during the flight, ask the doctor to write a letter (or fill out the airline-provided form) with informa-tion relevant to your parent's need for the device. (See chapter 3 for detailed information about traveling with a POC.) Finally, ask the doctor to write up a statement of any conditions or issues your parent has that another doctor should know about if your parent has to seek medical attention during your trip.

• If you haven't traveled with your parents in a while, find out what luggage they'll be bringing on the trip. After all, *you* may be the one who ends up carrying their suitcases around everywhere! I cannot stress enough the importance of having wheels on all luggage (both checked bags and carry-on ones). From experience, I can tell you that this vital feature is something you'll overlook only once. After you spend one vacation dragging carry-ons and heavy suitcases, the importance of wheeled luggage will be permanently etched on your mind (and you'll always remember to ask your parents about it).

• Now is also a good time to start mapping out the details of your itin-erary. Keep the daily pace to one your parents can manage, and make sure that the sites you're visiting have elevators, wheelchair accessibil-ity (and wheelchairs for rent, if you do not bring one from home or from your hotel), or whatever else your parents might need to help with their mobility issues. Also consider how you'll get from location to location. If your parent can't walk or can walk only short distances, for example, you'll need to investigate transportation options such as private cars, public transportation, or transportation provided by tour companies. My mom has to rest after walking one short New York City block (and she can walk only a few of those blocks before she's totally worn out), so I have a good idea of what pace she can handle. When we're on vacation, I want her to use her energy for walking around the tourist sites instead of for getting from place to place, so I typically rent a car for our exclusive use on our sightseeing days. I also love booking private tours through the hotel concierge, because these options give us control over the program—an important consideration if your parent has incontinence issues and you need to change your plans quickly.

One Week Prior to Departure

- If you're flying to your destination, confirm with the airline that it will indeed have a wheelchair waiting to get your parent through the airport. (This is a follow-up to the wheelchair assistance you requested when you originally booked the flight.) Many aging parents have trouble navigating airport sprawl and walking the long distance from the entrance to the departure gates for international flights. (Terminal 4 at JFK International Airport, anyone?) So arranging for wheelchair assistance is a great idea. Make sure to do this well in advance of a trip: although it *is* possible to request a wheelchair at check-in, booking it through the airline ahead of time ensures that your parent is met planeside with a wheelchair when you arrive at your destination—something that's particularly helpful when you have little time to get to the gate for a connecting flight. And here's another great reason to request wheelchair assistance: when going through customs, wheelchair users typically get to use a special lane that expedites entry.

- If you're traveling to a place where you don't speak the local language, make arrangements through the hotel for car service to meet you and your parent at the airport when you land. I find this the easiest way to deal with navigating a foreign city with Mom, especially when I'm exhausted after a long flight. Usually the driver handles the luggage once I'm through customs, which frees me to push Mom's wheelchair and get her settled in the car. Having prearranged private car service is so much more pleasant than dealing with local cabs that have hit-or-miss air conditioning, limited trunk space, and drivers who don't necessarily place a high priority on getting us to the hotel by the most direct route.

- Other tasks to take care of during the week before your trip include exchanging money (if you're going to a foreign country), completing a hold-mail request at your local post office or online at www.usps.com, suspending newspaper delivery, and paying bills that are due while you're out of town. You and your parents will also want to clear your calendars of any appointments (remind your parents to check in particular for any doctor's appointments) scheduled for while you're on vacation.

- This week is also a good time to finalize your financial plans for the trip—specifically, how you and your parents will pay for most things during your travels. You'll use cash for small purchases (e.g., a cup of coffee at a café), but you're likely to handle most of your expenses with either debit cards or credit cards. When traveling abroad, I much prefer the latter, because someone who steals your debit card number can clean out your bank account while you're on vacation— and straightening out that mess (and getting the money deposited back into your account) can take weeks. If someone makes unauthorized charges on your credit card, though, the company will usually credit you for them right away so you aren't out any money while it looks into the charges. For these reasons, I rarely use my debit card while traveling overseas, and I encourage you and your parents to do the same. That said, check with your credit card provider about whether it charges fees for foreign transactions. Many cards charge those fees, which can add up quickly. Make sure you discuss with your parents what credit cards they will be taking on vacation, and encourage them to bring only the bare minimum. (See chapter 10 for more information on managing your finances and valuables during your trip.)

- Speaking of bare minimums, have your parents clean out their wallets and purses and remove items they won't need for the trip. The fewer items they bring, the fewer items they might lose. Consider getting your parent a travel purse or travel wallet. These small, lightweight bags, available for both men and women, are designed to be pickpocket resistant and easy and comfortable to wear. Most can be slung over a shoulder or worn cross-body, and because they're worn on the torso, they are unlikely to be left behind while you're in transit and sightseeing. (My mom can sometimes feel a bit overwhelmed by all the new things coming at her when we're on vacation, and without a bag like this she might easily leave something behind when we stop for lunch or take a rest on a bench.)

- My mom can pack her bags in two hours if she has a checklist, but if your parents need a bit more time than that to pull their stuff together, now is the time to start helping them figure out what to bring. Talk to your parents about what clothes they'll need for your daytime activities and whether they should bring special attire for evening events, and help them identify anything else they'll need to feel prepared for all the adventures that await them. Sending your parents a checklist of items to bring (see appendix 2 for suggestions) can help them get their packing done efficiently—and with minimal stress.

- Because Mom worries about her house while she's away on vacation, one week out I remind her to ask her neighbor to keep an eye on it while she's gone. Doing this gives her tremendous peace of mind: knowing that someone is on the lookout for suspicious behavior around her house lets her relax and enjoy her vacation. Consider encouraging your parents to make similar arrangements with their neighbors.

Three Days Prior to Departure

- Follow up on any special requests (such as for exclusive use of a hotel wheelchair during your stay, for example) you made to your hotel by calling and asking to speak with the front desk manager, the person who's really in charge of guests' needs and requests when they are on-site. Because the general manager will typically forward requests to the front desk manager, speaking directly with the latter shortly before you arrive will let you confirm that your requested arrangements have been made.

- Make copies of the picture pages of your passports and of your credit and debit cards so that you have that information in case the originals are lost during the trip. Keep one hard copy in your carry-on luggage, ask a trusted friend to keep another hard copy, and keep an electronic copy in a location (such as Gmail, Yahoo, or another web-based e-mail service) that you can easily access from anywhere in the world in the event your original documents and your hard copies of them disappear.

- If your parents have any issues with swelling feet on long-haul flights, you may want to buy them some compression socks. Mom finds them uncomfortable to wear, so she doesn't use them; instead she props her feet up on the bulkhead, and we walk around the plane together every hour or so. I've heard lots of good things from folks who do wear them, though, so check to see if they're a good option for your parents. If they decide to give these socks a try, make sure they avoid off-the-shelf brands and instead get properly fitted for them at a medical supply facility.

- Mom's doctor recommends that she start a low-dose aspirin regimen a few days before travel to help reduce swelling in her feet on long-haul flights. The aspirin helps to thin the blood, which in turn improves her circulation. If your parents' feet are prone to swelling, they may want to ask their doctor about trying this themselves. It's critical that they do this only under a physician's supervision, though, because (among other possible complications) aspirin can react with other medications they take.

One Day Prior to Departure

- Review with your parents which items go in checked luggage and which (such as medications) must be hand-carried on the plane. Don't forget to pack snacks, especially if your parent is prone to hypoglycemia (low blood sugar).

- Bring copies of your parents' prescriptions in case questions about them arise when you go through security. (In the U.S., so far I've been questioned only when carrying a liquid prescription in a quantity that exceeds the usual allowable limit of 3.4 ounces. But I still bring forms for everything, no matter where I'm traveling. Better to be safe than sorry!)

- If your parent uses a hearing aid, pack extra batteries in your carry-on. (Nothing drives me crazier than Mom asking, "What? What?" when she can't hear the gate agent's announcements because her hearing aid batteries have died. Silly, I know, but it's the reality of traveling together. And that's why I never forget to bring spare batteries.)

- Bring along a magnifying glass and a pen light for reading on the plane. (The overhead lights offer only spotty coverage.)

- Most importantly, stock your carry-on with reading materials, games, crossword puzzles, or other items to entertain you and your parents during the trip and during any unexpected delays.

- Twenty-four hours prior to departure is the usual deadline for buying trip insurance. So if this is something you're interested in, now's the time to book it. Although some airports have kiosks where you can purchase trip insurance, I recommend taking care of this *before* you leave home so you have plenty of time to research the coverage you need. Be sure to bring a copy of the insurance policy with you, as well as a list of local hospitals at your destination. The insurer can typically provide you with this list based on your destination.

Day of Departure

- Double (and triple!) check that your carry-on bags contain all of your needed medicines, prescription details, passports, and medical information.

- Arrive early at the airport so you have plenty of time to check in and get through security. The wait times in security can be a nightmare, particularly during peak travel periods such as holidays.

- Also, if you've requested wheelchair assistance at the airport to get you to your departure gate, verify that "wheelchair assist" is printed on your airline boarding passes so you know that the airline has your request in its records.

Upon Arrival at Your Destination

- When you travel on your own, *you* may be able to go straight from the airport to the hotel to drop off your bags, and then out for some sightseeing. But that plan probably won't work for your parents. Aging parents usually take a bit longer to adjust to time changes and the effects of long flights, so plan on a bit of downtime—or at least slowed-down time—when you first reach your destination. After long-haul flights, I typically keep activities to a minimum for a day or two to give Mom time to recover from the stress of travel and to allow any swelling of her feet to subside. (Propping her feet up three times a day helps a lot with that.) That doesn't mean we don't do any sightseeing in those first few days. We just take it a bit easy so she has time to rest. If we've traveled across several time zones, we're also a little crabby at the end of our journey, so sleep is a good thing for both of us!

Pre-Trip Preparations for Traveling with Medical Items

If your parent needs to travel with any large, highly regulated, or other-wise out-of-the-ordinary medical items, you'll need to plan for them well in advance of your trip to ensure that you don't have any problems taking them to your destination. Your parent's doctor is a good starting point for infor-mation on the regulations for traveling with these items, but you'll likely have to do your own research as well. The resources section in appendix 1 offers some general starting points, and chapter 3 discusses at length how to travel safely (and legally) with one commonly transported device, a portable oxygen concentrator. This section focuses on a need that many seniors have: the need to travel with medications that require refrigeration.

When traveling with medications that must stay cold, you'll need a travel cooler specifically designed for this purpose. A regular cooler purchased at the local sporting goods store is inadequate, particularly if you're flying to your destination and experience any delays. Whoever provides the medicine to your parents may be able to provide a cooler or offer a recommendation on where to find one. Right before you leave home to begin your vacation, pack the amount of medicine you'll need for the number of days you'll be traveling, plus two additional days' worth to cover transit delays, along with the recommended quantity of ice packs and some zip-top bags.

If you're flying to your destination, do not pack prescriptions in your checked luggage; because baggage compartments are not temperature con-trolled, items in checked bags may be exposed to freezing temperatures that can adversely affect your medicines. The Transportation Security Adminis-tration (TSA) allows passengers to bring medically necessary liquids (with an accompanying prescription form) in carry-on bags, along with ice if the medicine requires refrigeration. Unlike other liquids, medically necessary liquids can exceed the TSA's limit of 3.4 ounces per container and do not have to be stuffed into a quart-size zip-top bag, though the TSA does usually require them to be in a separate container. Don't forget to bring the orig-inal packaging with your prescription label on it, because airport security and customs agents, both in the U.S. and abroad, will scrutinize any liquid medications you're carrying. If you use syringes to administer your medicine, you'll need a prescription form for them, too, as well as a sharps-disposal container. Be prepared for the TSA agents to look inside your carry-on and to examine your medicines. And to avoid delays at the security screening, be sure to declare them to the security agent before sending them through the X-ray machine.

If you're on a long-haul flight, speak with the flight attendant as you're boarding and ask about restocking the ice supply in your travel cooler during the flight. If there's room in the onboard refrigerator, you may even be able to stow your medicines—which should be clearly labeled before you leave home—in there. In that case, be sure to set an alarm on your phone or watch so you don't forget to retrieve them at the end of the flight.

When booking a hotel, ask about the availability of in-room refrigerators. If you are able to reserve a room with a fridge, make sure it's one that can hold your stuff and not one designed to hold only the hotel-provided beverages and snacks. If the hotel doesn't offer in-room refrigerators, ask the hotel staff about renting a suitable one for the duration of your stay or, if that isn't an option, see if you can store your medicines in the hotel refrigerator.

If you do store your medicines in the hotel's refrigerator, check to make sure that its lowest temperature won't adversely affect them. (Many hotel and restaurant refrigerators are set for low temperatures to mitigate the effect of the door being opened frequently.) Clearly label your containers with your name, contact information, and room number, and update that data for each hotel you stay in. Also make sure your labels include medical symbols so that anyone who comes across your package knows that it contains medicine that is both extremely valuable to its owner and something that should be kept separate from any fare served in the restaurant!

If you use an in-room refrigerator, be aware that in many hotels (particularly in Europe, but in other parts of the world as well), to turn on the room's electricity you'll need to insert your key in a slot located inside the room next to the door. If you want the electricity to stay on when you leave the room, you must leave a key in the slot at all times. However, know that the hotel cleaning staff might remove the key, and thus turn off the power, as part of their normal routine for cleaning and making up a room. Ask the hotel manager how electricity is managed in guests' rooms, and if it looks likely that the power will be out in your room while you're sightseeing, ask if you can store your medicines in the hotel's refrigerator during the day.

If you don't have access to any refrigerator at all, don't worry: with a little extra work on your part, you can still travel with medication that needs to stay cold. All you have to do is make ice packs with the zip-top bags you stuffed in your cooler on the day of your departure and periodically refresh the ice in them. If you're staying in a hotel, you'll have no trouble getting ice there, and if your vacation is a road trip (such as driving cross country by car), you can find ice at most gas stations and convenience marts.

Final Thoughts

After reading this chapter, I hope you're not feeling overwhelmed by the amount of planning that goes into taking a trip with an aging parent. Rather, I hope you're feeling inspired! Sure, there are lots of to-do lists to work through when preparing for this sort of trip. But none of the tasks is especially difficult, and all of them can be completed without too much stress if you spread them out (and don't wait until the last minute) and keep your eyes on the prize: a wonderful vacation full of great experiences that will help you and your parents strengthen your connection to each other!

6

CHECKING YOUR EMOTIONAL BAGGAGE WHILE ON THE ROAD

You just have to get rid of so much baggage to be light enough
to dance, to sing, to play. You don't have time to carry grudges;
you don't have time to cling to the need to be right.
—Anne Lamott

Over dinner one evening, my friend Dan mentioned that he was disappointed in his mother because she was afraid to fly to New York City to visit him. Dan quipped, "Here's a woman who marched on Washington to protest the Vietnam War, traveled solo to six continents, and raised her children single-handedly—and now she can't get on a plane by herself for a direct flight from Indiana to New York!" He was quite upset, and his comments drove home for me how much we fail to keep up with the emotional and psychological changes that happen to our parents as they age.

I'm guilty of this myself. My mom's house is surrounded by six acres of woods and rolling hills, and she and my dad used to work in the yard every day; their place looked like a manicured park! Since his death, though, she refuses to go out—even onto the back deck—because she's convinced someone is going to jump her. Who exactly that would be, she has no idea. She merely says, "People are lurking everywhere."

Like my friend Dan, I found myself frustrated and irritated at a parent for having such irrational (to me, at least) fears. I wanted Mom to break free of them, so of course I offered plenty of suggestions. Knowing that current events were a major source of her insecurities, for example, I told her, "Stop reading the paper and watching the news." (I still stand by those recommendations, even though she didn't follow them!)

Unfortunately, it took me *years* to accept the fact that Mom had changed. I finally realized that her fears were part of her now and that I needed to stop hounding her to venture into the yard. (In retrospect, I think some of my insistence on her going outside grew from concern that she'd become a shut-in. Thankfully that has not come to pass—she's out all the time with friends and activities!) I've come to accept that Mom going out on her deck or walking around her yard is not going to happen. I've had to let go of past expectations and adapt to a new norm.

Somewhere in the back corners of our minds, we're all vaguely aware that "things change as we age." But most of us haven't fully embraced that understanding, especially regarding our parents. Is it perhaps because admitting that our parents are aging means admitting that *we're* getting older too? (Honestly, that's not something I like to dwell on myself . . .) Or could it be that we've always thought of our parents as *our* caregivers and can't imagine that relationship ever changing? Or do we have trouble accepting any changes because of the inherent tension between parents and their children—the push-pull that never really goes away?

Just because your parents have changed and you have a different relationship with them now doesn't mean that you all can't have a blast together on vacation. Once you accept the new status quo, all you have to do is adapt to it. You have to walk into the situation with the right attitude—and the right techniques to talk yourself off the ledge when you get annoyed.

What to Expect

Mentally preparing yourself for the vacation must start on the day you decide to take your aging parent with you. Traveling is tough, even for the most seasoned road warriors among us. Even if your parents have done a lot of traveling in the past, they change as they get older, including in their ability to adapt to new cultures. Even the simple act of ordering a meal may be stressful to your parents, especially if they have to do so in a foreign country where the accented English (or completely different language) may be confusing to them. Unfortunately, stress leads to frustration. And because you are there and you are family—and the one who got them into this "situation"—you're probably the person your parent will take that frustration out on. Knowing this before you set out makes it easier to recognize (and deal with) when it happens.

It's also frustrating and disheartening to see your parents unable to make prudent decisions or act for themselves, particularly if they were in charge as you were growing up. Remember, in all aspects of life, whether it's the workplace or a shared vacation, change is stressful for *everyone*—even when it's change for the good. A vacation is a change in your parent's routine. Sometimes you'll need to reassure and cajole your parent to get him or her on board with the idea of taking a vacation at all, let alone the idea of traveling together. Is this extra effort worth it in the end? Absolutely—but only if you have the right mindset from the start.

Changes in a person's roles from childhood to adulthood also present an interesting dichotomy: some things change, but others never do. Although I'm now in my 40s, when I visit Mom in Indiana, she still asks the same questions that annoyed me when I was younger and living at home, such as "What time will you be home?" and "Can you call me if you'll be late?" and "Why do you choose *that* particular lipstick?" No matter how old I am or how our roles shift, I will *always* be Mom's little girl. I can't make her stop thinking like my mom, but I *can* change how I react to those questions. The issue here isn't one of her needing to trust me as an adult; rather, it's about me letting go of the emotional baggage that defines the parent-child relationship. So instead of being angry when Mom reminds me to "be careful" (aren't I always?), I try to remember to celebrate the fact that she still cares.

It's the emotional baggage, often tucked into the recesses of your mind, that you bring from your childhood that can make traveling together tough. So it's critical to adopt a philosophy of "letting go" when you're on vacation with an aging parent—or other family members, for that matter. If not, even a simple beach getaway can turn into a test of wills—deciding whether to sit in the sun or in the shade, choosing whether to spend the day by the pool or on the beach, etc. At any moment, we're a hairsbreadth from snapping at each other when someone offers a suggestion that differs from one already proposed. And the effect is usually strongest among family members: I've traveled extensively with both friends and family and am amazed at how I can take friends' suggestions in stride but regard those from Mom or another family member as negative judgments on my proposals. Yes, that's the emotional baggage I'm talking about—and that's what we have to manage somehow when we're "relaxing" together on vacation.

Emotional Triggers and Proximity

When I tell people how much I've traveled with my mom (300,000+ miles so far—and counting!), I usually hear a shocked response along the lines of "How could you spend that much time with your mom?" Even people who get along great with their parents are often aghast at the thought of traveling with them. When traveling with *anyone*, you'll spend a lot of time in close quarters together, and annoying aspects of everyone's personalities can burst forth. We all have hot buttons, but because of shared history, family members are the ones who best know how to push them—both intentionally and unintentionally. Now I won't kid you: traveling with Mom can be hard. After all, she's *still* my mother—and she *still* knows only too well what sets me off, just as I know how to send her over the edge! That said, outside of a few occasional minor conflicts, we truly enjoy each other's company and have come to a great place where we can both overlook the challenging parts of our personalities and get on with having a great vacation.

Be prepared for the "little" things to chip away at your positive attitude. It's the quick, petty comments that start to get on your nerves—complaints about cold dinner rolls ("Why don't they warm them up?"), the hardness of the butter ("How am I supposed to spread this on a cold roll?"), and anything that's unfamiliar ("Why don't they do things like we do it back home?"). As parents age, they can become less tolerant of cultural differences—a characteristic that can make a traveling companion a bit anxious when traveling overseas.

When you start to feel irritated, first remind yourself that you're *on vacation*. The goal—for both you and your parent—is to relax and get away from your regular routines. Second, try to shift the focus from the negative to the positive. Humor does the trick for me when I need to stop Mom from lamenting about how much more she likes how things are back home; I say, "Remember, you're *having a good time!*" This phrase never fails to get her laughing and reduces my tension level as well. Making light of annoying and uncomfortable situations helps keep Mom calm and having a good time—while also preventing me from losing my cool.

Techniques for "Letting Go"

On those unavoidable days when your buttons are pushed too hard, resist the urge to fight. Let it go—let go of being right, of having the last word, of proving how smart you are. After all, we're adults now, and part of being a grown-up is letting go. (Right?) So count to 10 quietly to yourself, leave the room, or close your eyes and take a deep breath. Here are a few more ideas on how to let go and get on with a great vacation.

Get Sleep

Nothing makes me crabby and quick to anger more than being tired. In fact, sometimes I can hardly stand to be around myself when I've fallen behind on sleep. Unfortunately, the same goes for my mom. So when we're both jet-lagged from flying halfway around the globe, it's best to avoid us during that first 24 hours!

Although many seasoned road warriors and travel sites say that the best way to ease the transition to a new time zone is to stay awake until the local bedtime, I prefer to listen to my body. If it's begging for sleep—particularly to the point where I'm feeling sick—I lie down for a quick snooze of 30 to 60 minutes. This little power nap does wonders for my attitude—and for Mom's, because she takes a nap too. Afterward, my nerves aren't as frayed, and my hot buttons don't get pushed as easily.

So prioritize sleep during your trip. Do what you can to catch some winks while en route—not always an easy task, since it's difficult to sleep in those uncomfortable airplane seats—and take care of yourself once you arrive at your destination. Making sure you're well rested will go a long way toward helping you keep your emotional baggage in check.

Don't Overbook

When I travel, I have a tendency to plan out every moment of the trip—and I do mean *every* moment. When Mom and I travel together, we inevitably fall behind on my carefully planned-out schedule. Then I start looking for where to pin the blame—and that's a mindset that leads nowhere good.

Let go of the goal to "see everything there is to see" in a city, and instead focus on enjoying and experiencing your new surroundings. Take the time to have a glass of wine at an outdoor café or enjoy a leisurely meal (including dessert!) at a restaurant you read about on the flight over. *Be in the moment* and let the world revolve around you.

Sure, you want to see and do lots of stuff. But you won't enjoy much of it if you run yourselves ragged. So plan downtime into your trip schedule, to give you and your parent opportunities to catch your breath and notice the rhythm of the city around you.

Plan Activities on Your Own

To help keep a positive mindset while on vacation, do some research before you go on your trip and identify activities that you and your parent can do together as well as activities that you can each do separately. Being in contact 24/7 while on vacation can tax even the best of relationships (Mom and I can attest to this!), so give each other a bit of space and some time alone.

On our trip to Australia, for example, I spent a day diving at the Great Barrier Reef while Mom hung out by the hotel pool and read, ate, and drank. We both had a marvelous day doing our own things. The time apart made our time together that much more special—and gave us a lot to chat about over dinner that evening!

Separate activities don't have to be all-day affairs, though. Sometimes all you need is an hour apart here or there. I typically take a walk by myself first thing each day before Mom is up and moving around, for example. Or in lieu of a walk, I visit a local coffee joint for an early-morning espresso before enjoying a leisurely breakfast later with Mom. Meal times have only slowed down with her as she's gotten in her 80s. Going to the gym is also something I'll do solo (Mom would *never* have an interest in joining me), and it's a healthy activity that lets me burn off calories (or stress) that may be building up.

Bring Along a Healthy Dose of Patience

You've probably heard the saying "Patience is a virtue." Before I started traveling with Mom, I wouldn't say that was part of my standard mindset. But now, whenever our plane races down the runway at the start of a new trip together, I remind myself to be the "Queen of Patience" with Mom and with all things on our upcoming adventure. I cannot change or control how other people—including my mom—will react. But I *can* make a pact with myself to be relaxed and patient while I am on vacation.

The key is to remember that when they're on a trip, your parents are out of their element and might need some extra time (and patience from you!) to handle all the temporary changes in their lives. As I pointed out in chapter 1, when I travel with Mom everything needs to s-l-o-o-o-o-w down. We start our day later, we take more breaks, and we stick to regular meal times (critical to maintaining Mom's pill schedule). We may visit fewer sites, but because pushing Mom in a wheelchair forces me to slow down, I end up seeing *more*. Rather than try to cram in loads of activities on a tight schedule, I get more in-depth experience at the few sites we do visit. Over time, I've come to realize that this relaxed pace lets both Mom and me better appreciate what we're seeing! And with a healthy dose of patience in hand, I don't mind the slower pace at all.

Pause Before You Speak

This is a tough one for me: as an extrovert, I tend to speak first and think later. I've found that consciously engaging my mind *before* opening my mouth has on many occasions stopped me from being a jerk.

If you find yourself feeling annoyed or frustrated or impatient or angry during your trip, keep the scream or mean words in your head. Instead, count to 10, then force yourself to slow down your speech as you engage your parent. This simple technique does wonders to silence the nasty comments before they escape from your mouth. Chances are you've probably seen this suggestion before, but in the heat of battle (especially if we're exhausted) we often forget the little things that can help us calm down. The more you practice self-calming techniques, especially before your trip, the better off you'll be when you need them.

To Engage or Not to Engage

Fortunately, Mom and I get along well. She's wonderful to be around. Although she can get nasty when she's tired (an attitude shift I see when I run her ragged, both at home and on the road), she's usually in a great mood.

We have a lot of fun together, and our mutual love of travel connects us. So when we're on the road, we're both in our happy place. Having such a positive start to our travels makes for better interactions during our vacation.

I realize, though, that each child has a unique relationship with his or her parent—and not everyone gets along. When I talk with my friends about some of their exchanges with their parents, I get a sense of how different parent-child relationships can be. And some of those situations they describe are so challenging that if I were in them, I'd have a hard time *not* engaging the parent—self-calming techniques be damned!

For ideas on how to work through interpersonal conflict with your parent while on vacation, take a look at these examples drawn from interviews I conducted with several people.

BRITTANY

When I first married, my relationship with my mother-in-law was far worse than it is now, because she had trouble accepting the fact that her son didn't need her any more. Over the years, though, I've learned ways to manage the challenges of this relationship, mostly by limiting the amount of time I spend with my in-laws.

If my husband and I are going to their house for an extended stay, for example, he will go for a longer period of time, and I'll pop in for a few days either at the beginning or at the end. He also vacations with them more often (say, twice a year), and I limit vacations with them to just one a year. When I'm there, I make sure to have some work-related materials with me, so when things get really bad I can excuse myself and go read—and my in-laws can't really complain, because this is stuff I have to do for my job. I also go to bed early and avoid situations where I'll be trapped with just my mother-in-law.

Minimizing the time I'm with them lets me not engage when she says something awful. I'll seethe inside, but I don't say anything. If I were around my mother-in-law more, I would need to engage her when she says mean things or is self-centered, because we would have to have better communication. But I don't see her enough to make it necessary for me to talk it out with her.

If you're in a team situation and have a partner or sibling who can run interference with the troublesome in-laws or parents, some of Brittany's techniques might work well for you. But what can you do when you have to deal with a parent alone, without an intermediary for the nastiness? In that case, you may want to follow the advice from Charles and Lindsey.

CHARLES

I recommended engaging your parents and calling them on the carpet if they are nasty to you. You definitely run the risk of escalating the situation, though, and I would be nervous about doing that while traveling, when screaming at each other (or stewing in silence) could ruin your precious vacation time. So consider taking this action well before the trip—to ensure that all the kinks have been worked out *before* you get on a plane together (or are trapped in a car for a horribly long drive!).

LINDSEY

One big change I've seen in my dad as he's gotten older is that he's become much more afraid. Rain, ice, going out at night, going to new places—all these things scare him now (and didn't used to before). We've traveled together in the U.S. and Italy, and it's been a big adjustment to travel with him when he's frightened. I know that when one of us is tired (especially after pushing too hard to explore lots of tourist sites), there's a greater chance that we'll snap at each other. So I try to be aware of his concerns and respect how he feels.

I've found that the best approach is to know the idiosyncrasies of your parents and recognize that at a certain point they've earned the right to be cranky and opinionated. There's no point in getting into an argument with them, because it's not a fight that you're going to win. You cannot change your parents, so why try?

Some of this advice might be helpful to you—or maybe it won't. Each relationship is different, and what works for Brittany and her in-laws or Lindsey and her dad might not work for you and your parent. You'll have to figure out the approach that's best for your situation.

Reading about others' experiences has made me appreciate my own parent even more. If my mom were over-the-top nasty to me, I would probably question whether or not I wanted to travel with her at all. At the same time, though, I might regard that as an indication that we both need to reconnect with each other and enjoy the remaining years in her life.

Overcoming Your Parents' Emotional Baggage

Lest you think that you're the only one bringing baggage to the party, don't fret: your parents surely have their own issues, especially if they can't do all the things they used to be able to do. As you get older, you probably get annoyed to find your body hurting in new places each year (I sure do!). Now try to see things from your parent's point of view. Imagine being excited to go on vacation and then realizing once you're there that you can't keep up. How frustrating would that be? This feeling is "excruciating," according to my mother, and it can cause her serious angst about vacationing with my brother and me if we let her stew on it—which we do not. We remind her that we *want* her along and that we're having a great time with her!

Here's one poignant example: a few years ago, Mom used a wheelchair for the first time. I had made arrangements for it without telling her—and she was not happy about it.

Val: What did you think when the Delta Airlines rep showed up with a wheelchair in Indianapolis Airport to wheel you to the gate when we were flying to China?

Mom: I was actually mad, and I couldn't believe you would do that without asking me first.

Val: If I had asked you, you would have said no.

Mom: Exactly! A wheelchair is for old people!

To my mom, wheelchair users are "old"—and who wants to admit to being *that*? Later, it became clear to me that her pride had been hurt: she didn't want to be seen as someone who couldn't make it on her own. (She *still* feels that way years later.)

I've learned from my experiences with Mom that a parent's reluctance to use a wheelchair is a *very* personal matter and one that you may have to address while on vacation together. The decision whether to use a wheelchair usually comes with plenty of emotional baggage, so I encourage you not to push your aging parent if he or she isn't ready to take this step.

If you think that your parents' mobility may be an issue during your trip, here are a few suggestions for tackling such a prickly topic with them:

- Review the list of possible trip activities with your parents, noting the physical activity level of each item. Get their input and pay particular attention to what excites them the most. If they're interested in an activity that's a stretch for their physical abilities, make arrangements to rent a wheelchair at that site. Once you arrive, mention to your parents that if they become fatigued, you can rent a wheelchair so they can get around easier and not miss anything.

  I used this approach the first time I rented a wheelchair for Mom at an attraction. I didn't mention her inability to keep up (and thus embarrass her), but I did say that I didn't want her to miss anything! She met this suggestion with resounding enthusiasm, because she hates the idea of missing something good even more than the thought of being in a wheelchair.

- Rent a wheelchair ahead of time and have it waiting in your hotel room when you arrive. This way, if your parent decides to use it, it's already there and readily available, rather than something you have to try to arrange at the last minute.

- If possible, rent an electric wheelchair rather than a push-from-behind model. It's like a car! And it gives your parents the freedom to go where they want without assistance. These chairs can go fast, though, so be prepared to jump out of the way quickly—or get hurt!

  Every time we've rented an electric wheelchair for her, Mom has accidentally run into me from behind. She's a speed demon in her car, and that attitude carries over when she's driving an electric wheelchair. The last time we were at Disney World, the staff there warned her several times to slow down. I was oddly proud of her for this—right up until she rammed me!

- Which member of your family does your parent listen to the best? People are often more receptive to feedback and requests from certain family members—and often unable even to consider suggestions from others. So if you want to encourage your parent to take a particular course of action, choose the messenger wisely!

  This is true in my family, and my brother and I use this knowledge as our secret weapon: if Mom refuses to do something (in the "we both know it's best for her, but she's being stubborn about it" category) that I've asked her to do, I ask my brother to step in, and invariably she'll listen to him. I'm not necessarily happy about this situation, but through the years I've lightened up a bit and learned to accept it as one of those "that's how it is" things. And ultimately, getting her to fulfill my request is more important than trying to avoid bruising my ego by getting my brother's help.

- When broaching the subject of using a wheelchair, do so privately. Don't put your parents on the spot in front of everyone and make a big (and public) deal about the fact that they cannot keep up.

- If your parent starts to falter while you're out and about, go get a wheelchair, bring it to where he or she is sitting, and mention something exciting that's around the corner: "Grab on, and let's go for a ride!" If you make using a wheelchair something fun instead of something that seems punitive, your parent may be more likely to give it a try.

- Most importantly, respect your parents' wishes. If they truly do not want to be in a wheelchair, don't force them to use one. They'll get there at some point—just perhaps not on this trip. Until then, consider finding a nice spot for them to sit and people-watch while the rest of you explore a site.

  My mom's interest in tourist attractions varies (she's so not into looking at temples or other religious sites), but she still wants to come along. Fortunately, she's as happy as a clam to hang out and people-watch on her own while the rest of us take our time checking out a site. This is a great option—and one I deploy at least once during every vacation with Mom.

Here are a few more non–wheelchair-specific thoughts to keep in mind as you plan your trip:

- I've mentioned this before, but it's worth repeating: avoid scheduling nonstop activities. *Everyone* (not just your parents) benefits from breaks and downtime during vacation.

- Plan the most physically strenuous activity for the time of day when your parents are at their peak energy levels.

- Contact the hotel before your trip and request the room closest to the elevator and the front entrance. There's no reason for your parents to wear themselves out just going to the lobby.

- If you're interested in activities beyond your parents' capabilities, discuss with them how they would feel if you went off on your own for a couple of hours while they hung out by the hotel pool or did some other low-key activity by themselves. This way their vacation can continue even when you're not there. Who knows—they might be happy to have some time to themselves!

When I'm off exploring on my own, Mom doesn't stay cooped up her in room but lounges by the pool or goes for a stroll around the hotel. If she's out for a short walk around the property and needs a break, she'll hang out on a bench and watch the people go by (a favorite pastime of hers, especially in new cities).

• Your parents will have a better time if they don't feel like they're burdens because they can't keep up. You've scheduled this time with them, so use it to relax and hang out together. Find great restaurants, for example, and enjoy long, delicious meals in each other's company. You both will probably enjoy those shared experiences as much, if not more, than spending time at the greatest of tourist sites!

These days, I prefer to travel light so I can avoid those annoying fees for checked luggage. If airlines could figure out a way to check my *emotional baggage*, though, I'd happily pay for that convenience! Unfortunately, airlines don't provide that service. So until they do, we all have to learn how to handle our emotional baggage ourselves. It's not as difficult as it seems, though. Pause, take a deep breath, and remind yourself how lucky you are to be alive and going on a trip with your parent.

GETTING THERE AND BACK

Stop worrying about the potholes in the road
and enjoy the journey.
—Babs Hoffman

As someone who travels more than 75,000 miles a year, I can confidently state that traveling *does* get easier when you do it on a regular basis. Traveling and preparing for a trip don't faze me at all, because I'm typically on the road at least two weeks out of each month. In fact, when I'm home for extended periods of time, *that's* when I start to feel antsy and uneasy!

For most people who don't travel often, though, change in routine can be stressful. Even *anticipating* the change can cause anxiety. Worrying about having to remember to bring both trip-specific items as well as daily essentials can rattle anyone, regardless of age. (My mom gets upset if she can't do a crossword puzzle each day, for example, so on our trips we *must* bring a book to work through together.)

Older adults, however, may experience more anxiety under those circumstances. As people age, they become less tolerant of change, which can heighten the tension around preparing to go. And once you and your parents hit the road, that stress can manifest in a variety of ways. Therefore, it's important to help your parents with their travel preparations so that getting there and back goes as smoothly (and as enjoyably!) as possible.

Whether you're flying, driving, or using some other means to get to your destination, here's the most important piece of advice I can give you for traveling with an aging parent: *expect delays.* If you're flying, your plane might not depart on time, you might miss a connection or two, and there's always a chance that your flight will be a nightmare full of crying babies, fighting passengers, or smelly feet. And if you're driving, you'll need to stop a lot more often than you anticipated, because bathroom breaks rarely occur at the same time as stops to gas up the car or eat. So adjust your usual expectations and allow more time than you think you'll need to get to your destination—and maybe even a bit of extra time for finding accommodations on the fly if your plans go awry. (I've had to do this with Mom on several occasions after we've missed connections.)

Although these sorts of challenges may sound like good reasons to stay home, *identifying* them in advance and being *prepared* for them will lessen the stress of dealing with them. For example, bringing items that can help smooth over any bumps you encounter during your trip can go a long way toward making the vacation more enjoyable for your parents—and for you, too. Here's a list of possibilities:

- Earplugs or headphones. (The latter are especially helpful if your parent wears hearing aids.)

- Healthy snacks, such as almonds or fruit bars. (These come in handy if your parent has low blood sugar, if he or she needs to eat before taking medicines, or if you miss a connecting flight late at night and all the restaurants in the terminal are closed until the next day.)

- Sanitary wipes and tissues.

- Reading materials, games, and a fully charged iPad (or similar device) loaded with movies. (The more entertainment options, the merrier!)

- A copy of the itinerary for your parent, so he or she won't have to keep asking you, "When will we get there?" (Honestly, I think Mom asks me that mostly to get revenge for all the times I pestered her with "Are we there yet?" when I was a kid!)

- Socks and a light jacket or blanket. (Many older adults find airplane temperatures too cold—and Mom is no exception. Heck, I get cold on planes, too!)

- Compression socks. (These aren't for everyone, though; see page 99.)

- Chocolate. (It's amazing how the pain of a flight delay can be eased with a treat! My mom has a little chocolate every night, so bringing some along on a trip has the added bonus of enabling her to maintain her daily ritual and therefore to feel a bit more comfortable when we travel.)

I would love to say that I rarely have to break out these items during our travels, but the reality is that because minor problems and inconveniences arise during every trip, it's pretty standard for Mom and me to use most (and sometimes all) of my "emergency supplies" while in transit. One great benefit to having this stuff on hand? Guilt-free binge-watching my favorite TV shows and reading gossip magazines! After all, when you're delayed in an airport, you have to do what you can to survive, right?

Preparing for an Unexpected Overnight Stay

Trying to predict the optimal traveling time based on the weather is like trying to win in Las Vegas: sometimes you come close, but success is usually just beyond your grasp. In Indiana, I grew up hearing, "If you don't like the weather, wait 10 minutes and it will change." That old saying pretty much describes what you're up against when you try to determine the best time to fly according to expected weather. Summer has thunderstorms, winter has ice, and spring and fall both bring a healthy mix of unpredictable weather. The difficulty of planning air travel based on weather patterns is further compounded by the fact that delays can result from weather conditions in multiple places: the airport you're flying from, the airport (or airports, if you don't have a nonstop flight) you're flying to, and the airport your plane is coming from. (Don't assume that your plane is coming from your destination airport. There's a good chance it's coming from a completely different location.) And with U.S. Department of Transportation regulations fining airlines for excessively delayed flights, when inclement weather is an issue, airlines often prefer to cancel a flight altogether rather than risk a heavy fine.

That brings me to a little travel secret that has saved me more times than I can remember: before Mom and I leave home on a trip that involves a flight with connections, I make a list of the names and phone numbers of the hotels closest to the airport. If we miss a connection due to weather or other factors, I'm ready to start dialing to find available rooms for the night. It's critical to gather this information ahead of time for two reasons:

- Some airports have courtesy phones that dial directly to nearby hotels. If a flight gets canceled, though, by the time you make your way to them you'll usually find only a few phones—and dozens (if not hundreds) of passengers queueing up to use them. With your trusty list and your cell phone, you can avoid that hassle completely.

- If the delay is caused by weather, the airline has no legal obligation to provide or pay for accommodations for stranded passengers. Airlines often try to help passengers locate rooms (and in this case, having preferred status with an airline might get you more of its staff's attention), but don't count on their assistance—and don't expect a discounted room price, either. Arguing with the agents on duty probably won't accomplish much, because their hands are tied by company policies, and they'll usually instruct you to send your complaints to the corporate office. So it's a better use of your time to focus on finding a room on your own—and then writing that complaint letter from the comfort of your hotel rather than from a chair in the airport terminal.

Keep in mind that even if the airline does cover your room for the night, it doesn't mean it's the best option for you. Those accommodations will usually be located far from the airport, because distance from the airport lowers the room cost (and airlines are always looking for a good deal). And that's another reason why you're usually better off arranging your own accommodations in the event of an overnight delay.

When calling around for available rooms, I prefer to find one as close to the airport as possible, even if it comes with a high price tag. (I make sure that my list includes each hotel's phone number as well as its distance from the airport and whether a shuttle is needed to get there.) If Mom and I are unexpectedly delayed overnight, we usually have a ridiculously early flight out the next morning. Getting as much sleep as possible is important when traveling with Mom, and a long shuttle ride to an off-airport hotel cuts into her rest time. Plus, having to navigate the shuttle's stairs can be particularly rough for her if we've just gotten off a long flight: Mom's legs retain water under normal circumstances, and after spending four or more hours on a plane it's even worse. At that point, she *really* needs to prop up her legs for 15 minutes before hitting the sack, and a short commute from the airport to the hotel lets her get to that sooner.

Although putting together a hotel list may seem like wasted effort if your flights stay on schedule, when they don't I promise you'll be weeping tears of joy when your parents have a place to lay their heads for the night—and it's not on your lap in a deserted terminal! For many aging parents (including my mom), their days of camping at the airport are long behind them. They're long gone for me, too, but if I have to sleep in an airport overnight, I can do it without serious consequences. For Mom, on the other hand, this could cause physical problems and could negatively affect her ability to handle the next day's travel. Trust me: if you do your homework so that you're prepared for problems that can arise when connecting in airports both in the U.S. and in other countries, you'll never regret it.

Easing the Stress of Flying

In addition to being prepared for an overnight stay due to flight delays, you can take other steps to make the whole in-transit part of your trip pleasant for your parent. (And when your parent is less stressed, *you* are less stressed. Everyone wins!) Here are a few examples of things I do when traveling with my mom. This list can serve as a starting point for your own list based on your parent's particular needs and preferences.

- Because of a condition called neuropathy, Mom's knees and legs ache constantly—and this discomfort worsens if her legs swell from sitting on a plane for long periods of time. So when booking plane tickets for our mother, my brother and I arrange for the highest level of service we can afford so she can either stretch out her legs or elevate them on a footrest. My elite status on Delta Airlines allows me to prebook economy comfort seats (with extra legroom and incline), which work well for many of Mom's flights. For long-haul flights, however, my brother and I decided several years ago that we would book Mom in business class, which has fully reclining seats and footrests that help reduce the swelling in her feet and minimize her discomfort.

- To find the best plane ticket fares (especially if we're planning to fly business class), I start looking well in advance of when we want to travel and try to remain flexible on departure and arrival dates. That said, figuring out when airfares will be at their lowest is as difficult as getting Congress to agree on something! For our last trip to China, I utilized several websites to monitor airfares for a few months before finally pulling the trigger and purchasing tickets eight months before our trip. Not only did Mom and I score pretty good prices, but we had months to pay off the tickets before incurring additional expenses during the trip.

- To minimize Mom's anxiety about going on an extended trip, I try to fly to her hometown of Indianapolis a couple of days early so I can help her with last-minute tasks such as packing and navigating the airport. For a short trip or one within the U.S., we can typically make do if she forgets anything; even if she forgets her medication, her doctor can arrange an emergency refill. For long-haul trips or those to international destinations, though, helping Mom with her pre-trip preparations becomes more critical because it's harder (if not impossible) to replace her medications overseas. Finding overseas replacements for nonmedical items, too, can be difficult due to lack of availability of similar products and, for clothing, proper sizes. (Don't underestimate the importance of making sure your parent brings enough critical clothing such as underwear or shirts. Mom has forgotten to bring both of them when traveling with me!) I don't meet Mom in Indiana before *every* trip we take together, because sometimes it's more convenient, and significantly less expensive, for us to meet in a connection city. In this event, I try to arrive first so I can greet Mom as she disembarks from her plane, and together we jump on the same plane to our final destination. But if your parent hasn't flown in a while, hasn't gone on a long-haul trip before, or seems hesitant about traveling, see if you can go to his or her hometown a few days before the trip so you can help with last-minute tasks—and help decrease his or her anxiety about the trip.

- During long-haul trips, try to break up long transit periods by staying a night or two in a connection city. This recovery time between flights has had quite a positive effect on my mom. I can power through a long journey, but Mom benefits from a break to prop up her feet and chill out. If your parents have any sort of circulation issues, as my mom does, giving them a break becomes even more critical for their well-being.

- I *always* reserve a wheelchair—and confirm it two weeks before our flight—for any time we spend in an airport. This enables Mom to ride in a wheelchair to our departure gate, from the plane to a connection gate, and from the final arrival gate to the airport exit. I do this at every airport (even small ones, such as Indianapolis International), because to someone who has difficulty walking, covering even short distances can feel like scaling Mount Kilimanjaro! So let your parents save their energy for touring the sites rather than spend it hiking from one end of the airport to the other.

- To me, this is an obvious thing to do, but I think it's worth mentioning anyway because it might not be obvious to everyone: book side-by-side seats when traveling with your parents. Mom is more comfortable when I'm near her, and being next to each other lets us plan how to handle flight delays that might come up. When I sit next to Mom, I'm also well positioned to help her stay entertained (and therefore happy) during the flight. I always bring tons of things to do when I'm traveling on my own, and when we travel together I consider it my job to make sure Mom has plenty of options as well—crossword puzzles, books, podcasts, audiobooks, etc.

Avoiding Deep Vein Thrombosis

Long plane rides *can* be fun. The movies, the snacks, the interesting seatmates . . . you never know *what* might happen! But flights can also have downsides—particularly when they present health risks to older folks. One of these risks, deep vein thrombosis (DVT), is a condition in which a blood clot forms in the deep veins of the legs. Because high altitude, dehydration, and lack of movement all contribute to the onset of DVT, it's often linked to airplane travel and has been nicknamed "economy class syndrome." *The risk of DVT increases dramatically after a long-haul flight.* So if your trip includes airplane travel segments that are longer than a couple of hours, be prepared to take steps—literally!—to keep DVT at bay. Walking the length of the plane every 90 minutes or so is your best strategy (although that's not always possible if the seat belt sign is illuminated), as is extending your calf and foot muscles regularly. Here are some exercises you can do in your seat to help avoid DVT.

- **Ankle turns:** Lift your feet from the floor and rotate one ankle clockwise and the other counterclockwise for 20 to 30 seconds. Switch directions and repeat.

- **Foot lifts:** Plant your feet on the floor, then keep your heels on the ground and lift your toes as high as they can go. Bring your toes back to the floor, then keep the balls of your feet planted while you lift your heels up. Repeat 10 times.

- **Knee lifts:** With your knees bent and your feet flat on the floor, raise one leg while tightening your thigh muscle, then lower it and do the same with the other leg. Repeat this movement 10 times for each leg.

- **Leg extensions:** Bring one knee up to your chest, then straighten your leg as far as it can go under the seat in front of you. Repeat 10 times. (Ideally, the area under the seat in front of you should be kept open so you can stretch your legs during the flight. As people bring more—and larger—carry-on bags, though, under-seat areas often fill up. In that case, you and your parent can take turns holding your under-seat bags in your laps while the other person does the stretches.)

- **Foot presses:** Every hour or so, press the balls of your feet down hard on the floor or footrest. This helps to increase the flow of blood in your legs.

Compression socks can help some people avoid DVT, so check with your doctor about this option. (And if he or she does recommend using these socks, be sure to get them fitted properly—don't just buy a pair off the shelf at the drugstore.) Elevating legs also helps with circulation, so if your seat has a footrest, be sure to use it.

Talk with your parent's doctor about whether your mom or dad should take a low-dose aspirin or other anticoagulant that helps to thin the blood and prevent DVT. (For example, my mom's doctor has her add this regimen to her pill schedule two days before flying.) Don't start this on your own, though. Always consult with a doctor to ensure these substances don't interfere with any other medicines your parent is taking.

Finally, it's also a good idea to avoid dehydration, which contributes to DVT, by laying off the in-flight alcohol and drinking water instead. I know that's not as much fun as having a glass of wine or a martini, but it's probably a wiser decision in the long run. I wouldn't say that Mom and I always follow that rule to a T ourselves, especially because she hates drinking water. So I usually strike a bargain with her: she can have a glass of Bailey's as long as she drinks a glass of water with it. I follow these rules too, and we make this into a fun game that we play together. After all, a partner makes everything much more fun—even hydrating ourselves!

Getting through Security as Painlessly as Possible

You've made all your reservations, packed your bags, and arrived at the airport well ahead of your scheduled departure time. One major hurdle remains: the dreaded security line. I think it's safe to say that no traveler hopes to encounter a long line at airport security. Waiting patiently until you finally make it to the front, where you suddenly must *hurry up* and unpack and strip down, then repack and dress in seconds while the person behind you grumbles about the possibility of missing his or her flight—now *that's* a recipe for stress!

Those of us who travel frequently have the rhythm down pat: take off shoes, belt, and jacket; remove laptop from carry-on bag and place it in a bin; put clear plastic bag with containers of liquids into the bin. If I'm by myself, the experience is usually quick and painless. However, when I travel with Mom or with my toddler nieces, it's a completely different story. Here are a few tips for getting through airport security as quickly and painlessly as possible.

Arrive Early

It *is* possible to make it through the security screening with your aging parent—and without losing your mind. I do it all the time with my mom in her wheelchair. Here's the most important advice I can give for making this process as painless as possible: *get to the airport early*. Arrive at the airport a good two hours before your flight so you have plenty of time to get through that line. (Two hours is ideal, but if you can't manage that, allow a minimum of 90 minutes.) Arriving shortly before your scheduled departure guarantees an extremely stressful wait at security and the possibility of missing your flight, neither of which is a good way to start a journey. Trust me, if you follow only one piece of my advice, make it this one, because it is *incredibly* stressful to try to get through security when you're in a hurry.

Follow the TSA Rules

Read the latest travel rules and regulations on the Transportation Security Administration website (www.tsa.gov). Here's some great news for older travelers: as of January 2014, special screening policies are in effect for people over 75, such as no longer having to remove shoes or light jackets at the security screening. Special considerations aside, though, here are some best practices that *all* travelers should follow when going through security:

- Have your boarding pass and identification handy and ready for inspection.

- Remove your shoes and place them on the X-ray machine belt. (Travelers 75 or older are exempt from this.)

- If you're wearing a sweater or jacket, take it off and put it through the X-ray machine. (Travelers 75 or older are exempt from this, as are travelers who've opted into the TSA's PreCheck program, which offers expedited screening for approved travelers.)

- Empty your pockets. Place your wallet, belt, keys, change, cell phone, and bulky jewelry in a bin.

- Place your plastic zip-top bag of liquids in a bin.

- Take your laptop out of its bag and place it in a separate bin.

- Don't put wrapped gifts in your carry-on. If a security officer has to check that item, he or she won't hesitate to unwrap it.

Be sure to follow the TSA's rules about how to pack liquids, gels, and aerosols. I've covered these in detail elsewhere for general items (chapter 3) and for medications that require refrigeration (chapter 5). To avoid some of these hassles at the security screening, sign up for the TSA's PreCheck program (see below).

Request Assistance for Disabilities or Medical Conditions

If you or your traveling companions have any disabilities or medical conditions, be sure to request the services (such as wheelchair assistance) that can help you get through security and the rest of the airport more smoothly. The TSA doesn't provide such services, but airlines often do. The page "Travelers with Disabilities or Medical Conditions" on the TSA website has plenty of helpful information on this topic; if you have questions about screening policies and procedures or about what to expect at the security check, call the TSA Cares help line at 1-855-787-2227. If you need assistance going through security checkpoints, be sure to call the TSA at least 72 hours before your flight to allow time for planning the needed support.

Consider Enrolling in TSA PreCheck

The TSA PreCheck program lets preapproved travelers apply for expedited screening at participating U.S. airports. Approved travelers are issued a Known Traveler Number (KTN), which lets them enjoy shorter lines at security—and they don't have to take off their jackets or shoes or remove laptops and bags of liquids from carry-ons. If you're a frequent traveler, it may be worth the extra time (which includes visiting an enrollment center located at larger airports) and money ($85) to apply for PreCheck approval.

Don't Joke!

I know I don't need to say this to most of you, but it bears repeating just in case: if you or your traveling companions have a rebellious sense of humor, *do not* make any inappropriate travel-security–related jokes at a security checkpoint—or anywhere in an airport or airplane, for that matter. The TSA takes that stuff seriously! So keep a lid on those jokes until you're at your destination or home. Otherwise you may spend *a lot* more time at the airport than you had originally planned . . .

Relax!

Getting through airport security efficiently and easily may seem a daunting task. But the process can be made more bearable if you give yourself plenty of time and are aware of the general rules. If you or your parent find yourselves feeling stressed out, take some deep breaths and remember that you'll soon be through the checkpoint and on your way.

Traveling by Car

Once you reach your destination, you may decide to use a car (a rental if you've flown there, or your own if you've driven) to get around town. This situation presents its own challenges, and I've compiled a list of practical recommendations drawn from my many experiences with renting and driving cars when Mom and I travel together. This section covers logistical considerations (see chapter 10 for information on car-rental insurance issues). In general, the key is to manage as much of the car parking and retrieval as you can on your own so your parent doesn't have to walk long distances.

Rental Cars

- Trips involving a rental car present unique logistical challenges, because car pickup locations are typically far from airports and reachable only by shuttles. Getting from the airport to the car rental office can be especially difficult when traveling with an aging parent: shuttle drivers rarely help load and unload luggage, and climbing in and out of the shuttle van or bus (vehicles that usually have high steps) can be exhausting for seniors, particularly when they're already weary after spending a lot of time on planes and in airports.

- After you've collected your checked luggage, leave your parent and all the luggage in the airport while you take the shuttle to the car rental office and pick up your car. There's no need for *both* of you to make that trip!

- Before leaving the airport, help your parent find a comfortable place to sit (e.g., an outside bench in warm weather, a chair next to a window in cold or rainy weather) where he or she can see you when you arrive. Make sure it's near a spot where you can bring the car up close for loading your parent (and your luggage). Getting a ticket for parking too long or in the wrong place is a terrible way to start a vacation!

- When it's time to fly home, drop your parent and the luggage off at the airport, then return the car to the rental agency by yourself before riding the shuttle back to the airport. (You'll have to budget some extra time for this, but your parent will surely be happy not to have to make that trip.)

All Cars

- In a sprawling city such as Los Angeles, a car is probably the best way to get around, because cab rides over long distances will cost you an arm and a leg. But in denser cities (which often have hard-to-navigate narrow streets and limited public parking spaces), you may be better off leaving the car at your hotel and using cabs for short trips around town.

- When you do take your car for an outing (to a restaurant, theater, or museum, for example), call the destination ahead of time to find out if it offers valet parking. It's not free, but the cost may be worth the savings in stress from trying to find a parking space!

- If valet service isn't an option, drop your parent off at the door and park the car yourself. When it's time to leave, retrieve the car by yourself and pick up your parent at the door.

If you or your parent qualifies for a handicapped parking placard, find out *before* your trip what you need to do to use one during your trip. Sometimes you can use your regular placard on a rental car, and sometimes you may have to obtain one that's specific to your location (if you're traveling to a different state or country, for example). *Always* verify the regulations in advance, and don't make any assumptions about what you're allowed to do. Wading through the bureaucracy to find this information can be a bit of a pain, but if it makes it easier for your parent to access your car because you're able to park in a handicapped spot near the door at your destination, the effort is well worth it.

Final Thoughts

I've covered a lot of ground in this chapter, I know! But none of the tips I've mentioned is particularly difficult to follow. Because they aren't part of your regular routine, though, some of them might be easy to overlook without a reminder here and there. But if you plan ahead, take your time, double-check everything, and take a deep breath every once in a while, you and your parents can avoid a lot of the stress often associated with travel and instead focus on enjoying your great adventure together!

ACTUALLY ENJOYING
YOUR VACATION

Enjoy today because yesterday is gone and
tomorrow is never promised.
—Anonymous

Ahhhh—you're finally on vacation! After months of prepping, days of packing, and hours in transit, you've arrived at your destination and you're ready to enjoy the fruits of your labor. Fortunately, the vacation itself is the easiest part of this whole process.

To ensure that both you and your parent have a good time during your trip together, make sure that you both stay well rested, well fed, and well entertained. Key elements of any great vacation—and especially one with an aging parent—include catching up on sleep (a luxury few of us have in our everyday lives), enjoying plenty of great food and beverages (without having to clean up the dishes afterward), and partaking in a nice mix of activities such as reading, relaxing, and sightseeing, depending on your parent's physical capabilities and your shared interests. Whatever you decide to do, it's important to figure out a rhythm that works best for you and your parent and helps you make the most of your time together. Remember, though, that you and your parent may have different styles, so be prepared to make compromises and find a middle ground.

As someone who loves to plan (I'm a project manager from way back, so calendars and to-do lists make my heart leap for joy!), I meticulously schedule my daily action items when I'm at home—a tough habit to break when I'm on vacation. But my mom doesn't share that perspective. She doesn't care to adhere to a fixed timetable or to see every church, historical location, or obscure attraction (the world's largest ball of twine, anyone?) in a particular place. She mostly wants to spend time with my brother, his family, and me. Clearly, Mom and I have different goals while on vacation. So we've learned how important it is for us to find the intersection of our differing interests and abilities.

If your parent can hike Mount Fuji, that's fantastic. (A strenuous activity like that is not for *my* mom, though—and it's not for *me*, either!) Understand, though, that as people age, their energy levels change: they can diminish, shift to different times of the day, fluctuate, or undergo other changes. In addition, keep in mind that your parent's energy levels may vary greatly from yours—and you'll need to accommodate those differences. For example, you may need to schedule more breaks throughout the day or take it easy after you've done an activity together. (My mom can go only so long before she needs an entire day to chill out and relax.) Remember, change is hard even when it's part of an awesome vacation. And because seniors often find change worrisome, when they're on vacation and in unfamiliar settings they can tire more quickly than they usually do at home.

So if traveling together is so stressful, why do it? Travel enables people to connect with each other in deeper and more meaningful ways. Sometimes the challenge of handling change can serve as the glue for this bonding experience. As fellow travelers, you and your parent may feel united against the world (at least when you're trying to figure out street signs in a foreign language!), and if you can take in stride (and with a sense of humor) the challenges you encounter when traveling, you and your parents will be well on your way to having a fantastic experience together!

Talking to Your Parent

Here's a challenge to everyone traveling with a parent (or another family member or friend, for that matter): *put down the phone and talk to the person you're with.* I know—what a crazy concept! But so few people actually talk with each other anymore! We're so accustomed to using our phones for communication (via texts, e-mail, instant messages, etc.) that it's almost unheard of to put them away and actually speak with one another.

Make this trip the vacation where you truly connect with the people you're with. Remember that your parents won't be around forever, so use this time to learn more about them while you still have the chance. What were they like when they were little? Did they like school? What were their favorite jobs? Did their lives turn out the way they planned? What's on their list of places they want to explore, things they want to do, and activities to tackle? What were their favorite hobbies when they were growing up? Do they like fishing? (During a trip together last year, for example, I found out that my mom loves football and opera. I had no idea!)

Prepare for a trip with a parent as if you were preparing to conduct a job interview. Ask yourself what you already know about your parent and what is left to discover. Take the time to think about the questions that you will wonder about when your parents are no longer with you, and in what precious time you have left together treat them as your equals and explore their hopes and dreams. My father passed away unexpectedly several years ago, leaving me with so many questions about his childhood—and now the opportunity to find answers to them is gone forever.

We all want to be respected and heard. Because so much of society marginalizes the elderly, asking your parents meaningful questions and truly listening to their answers will go a long way toward reassuring them that they still matter to someone. Think about how often we get mad at our spouses, partners, children, and friends for taking us for granted. Your parents experience that, too, so make sure they *know* that you care about their lives.

You'll be surprised by what you can learn about your parents when you travel together and spend a lot of time in each other's company. During one of my early trips with Mom, for example, I learned that she had been kicked out of school for "roughhousing" (*my* mom—really?) and that my father briefly lost his license after flying his plane down the alley behind her parents' house when she told him she "wouldn't marry him if he was the last S.O.B. on earth." (Fortunately, she later changed her mind!) When you're relaxed on vacation, it's amazing what stories your parents (and perhaps you!) will tell. This is what traveling together is all about: connecting with each other while you still have the opportunity to do so.

One great thing about travel is that it gives you plenty to discuss with your parent. After all, whether you're headed to the next town over or to a city on the other side of the world, a new locale always offers surprises and variations on familiar things. For example, Mom loves chicken (it's her go-to dish when eating out), so whenever we travel we always try local chicken dishes and marvel at how the simple chicken can taste so different in other parts of the world—and even in other parts of the U.S. Going somewhere new lets you explore other cultures and discuss with your traveling companion how they differ from, and are similar to, your own. So if you find yourself at a loss for what to chat about with your parent during your trip, turn to your surroundings for inspiration and talk about what reminds you of home—and what you wish you could bring home with you!

Managing Your Expectations

When I go somewhere new, I like to visit the tourist sites there. (After all, if all the tourists are flocking to it, there *must* be a good reason to go see it, right?) To increase my efficiency at cramming in activities, I maintain two lists of things I want to see. The first includes big attractions that are either complicated to get to or require at least four hours to explore. The second list contains smaller sites that are a short cab ride from my hotel and won't take that long to check out.

I typically space out the big destinations so Mom and I visit one every other day; this pace gives her time to rest between excursions. On her rest days I often visit a site from my second list, checking with Mom if she wants to go with me or if she'd rather stay at the hotel. Most of the time, she opts to tag along, even if she's not interested in what I'm going to see. So I'll find a bench for her at or near the entrance so she can people-watch (something she loves to do) while I'm gone for an hour or so. On days when she decides to stay at the hotel, I'll help her find a place to hang out for a while by herself, such as under an umbrella next to the pool.

As you start to plan the activities for your trip with your parent, keep the following things in mind:

- When you first arrive at your destination, don't run out to start exploring right away—schedule time for both of you to rest first. If you're arriving in the early morning after an overnight flight and well before the hotel's official check-in time, pay the half-day fee so you can get into your room as soon as you arrive. Don't try to force an exhausted parent to stay up until the typical afternoon check-in time. Think about how awful you feel (and, if you're like me, what a bear you are to be around) when you're tired. The same—or even worse!—holds true for your parent.

- When you visit sites, use the form of transportation that's most comfortable for your parent. Public transportation is typically the lowest-cost option but can be the hardest one for aging parents to use. For example, the subway in New York City (where I live) is a great way for me to get around, but it has a lot of stairs that Mom can't manage—and only one-quarter of the subway stations are wheelchair accessible. So when she visits me, we get around by taxi or car service (cabs can be challenging to find when it's raining).

- Private tours that let you set your own pace are *lifesavers*! Yes, they are more expensive than regular tours. But the flexibility you get with a private tour can't be beat. I love them because when my travel group includes four adults (including one octogenarian) and twin toddlers, someone *always* needs to stop to use the bathroom. Traveling on a big tour can be incredibly nerve-wracking because of the pressure to keep up with the rest of the group. (Usually, these groups aren't happy about delays when the toddlers need a diaper change or Mom needs a rest.) So make exploring the sites easier for you and your parent by hiring a van and driver. It will be one of the best things you've ever done—I promise!

- Rent a wheelchair when possible. Having one will open so many possibilities! In the beginning, getting Mom to use one was a little dicey. But thank goodness she's no longer sensitive about feeling "old" because she needs a wheelchair. She knows that she'd tire much sooner without it, so now she sees it as a tool that lets her spend more time exploring the sites.

- Always pack snacks and water when exploring. *Always.* Fortunately, Mom doesn't have blood-sugar issues, but whenever we go out I have a snack at the ready just in case. A small bite to eat can be an amazing pick-me-up when Mom's energy levels are flagging and she's starting to fade.

- When planning to do big activities with set entry or start times, book plenty of downtime prior to the activity to ensure that your parent does indeed have enough energy to attend. Depending on what your parent needs, this downtime might mean doing nothing at all on the day before a big activity!

If you want to enjoy yourself while on vacation with a parent, you'll need to manage your expectations—and be flexible. You may have grandiose plans for all sorts of things to see and do together, but you need to be prepared for the possibility that one morning your parent will wake up and not feel up to going anywhere that day, preferring instead to take it easy at the hotel. The best way to handle this sort of change in plans is to go with the flow. Letting your parent's needs set the tone and pace of your travels will make things much easier for both of you.

At home, your parents are probably accustomed to moving at a much slower pace, so the hustle and bustle of tourist sites can wear them out. Make things a bit more comfortable for them by breaking up activities and scheduling downtime. Even if you've planned on a slow pace for your trip, be prepared for everything to come to a full stop if your parents need to chill out for a day. Finally, keep in mind that the travel "rhythm" you share with your parent will change every year and with each vacation. (As Mom's gotten older, for example, she needs more—and longer—breaks between activities.) So you'll need to keep making adjustments to that rhythm to find what works best for the two of you and helps you make the most of each other's company.

Planning Activities

Obviously your parents' physical abilities will influence what activities you can do together while on vacation. Even if your parents have slowed down with age, though, you don't necessarily need to rule out all strenuous activities, because there are services out there that can help your parent participate in even those situations.

For example, when Mom and I visited the Angkor Wat temple complex in Cambodia, we hired someone to push her around the site in a wheelchair and a second person to help carry the wheelchair up the steps so she could get a closer look at the ruins and explore that historical site. One friend of mine hired professional wheelchair pushers to help her parent make it around the entire 109 acres of Tiananmen Square. When you ask for help, it's amazing how much you can find!

Before you plan out your entire vacation schedule, in addition to considering your parents' abilities, be sure to ask your parents if there is anything they want to see or do in the area you'll be visiting. Remember, it's *their* vacation too, and they may have ideas for local activities. While planning our trip to Hawaii, for example, I asked Mom what she wanted to do there. Here's how she responded:

- See volcanoes via helicopter. (This was at the top of my list too! Unfortunately, weather prevented us from doing this, much to our disappointment.)

- Drive the road to Hana. (Before planning our trip, I didn't know what this was, but Mom knew she had to do it.)

- Visit Waikiki. (Mom wanted to follow in the footsteps of the Brady Bunch!)

- Visit Maui. (Mom saw Oprah take her staff there.)

If your parents don't have any particular ideas in mind, I recommend compiling a list of activities and then getting their input on it. Finding out what your parents *aren't* interested in doing can also help you put together a list of activities you can do on your own, such as during a "downtime" day when your parents want to relax at the hotel.

Visiting local points of interest is one possible activity to do while you're on vacation. Here are a few other ideas for things you and your parent can do together, regardless of your destination:

- If your parents love to read, vacation is a great opportunity for them to catch up on any books that have been sitting around their house for a while. (My mom always underestimates the number of books she'll go through on vacation and starts to get a little restless when she runs out of reading material. So at the start of our trip I like to surprise her with two books that I know she'll enjoy. I couch them as "bon voyage" gifts, knowing full well she'll need—and read!—them before the trip is through.) Audiobooks are a terrific option for anyone with eyesight issues. Don't forget to bring standard headphones if your parents wear hearing aids, because earbuds won't work with other in-ear devices. If you and your parents share a love of reading, you could also plan to read the same book while on vacation, then discuss it together at the end of the trip. (Think of it as your own little book club!)

- Playing games is a great way to socialize and relax at the same time. Perhaps it's time to learn pinochle or another card game (does your parent have a favorite?) the two of you can play together. In addition to a deck of cards, I also bring Jenga, a game that Mom and I both adore.

- Mom loves doing crossword puzzles, and though that isn't my favorite activity when I'm on my own, I do enjoy working on them with her. Finishing one together gives us both a real sense of excitement!

- Use your vacation as an opportunity to catch up on sleep. You can't turn on the television or pick up a newspaper these days without seeing stories explaining how getting at least eight hours of sleep each night can help you look younger, lose weight, and be more creative. In everyday life, though, getting a full night's rest is often easier said than done. So during your vacation, see if it's possible to get eight hours of sleep per night (can you shut your mind off for that amount of time?) and find out how it feels to do so for an entire week.

- Bring journals for both your parent and yourself. Even though I love to write (obviously!), I usually do a lot more business writing than personal journaling when I'm at home. So I love to use travel time to jot down my own thoughts and goals. Perhaps your parent would enjoy keeping his or her own travel journal too.

- Bring a scrapbook, glue, and tape. Although I make a photo scrapbook for her several weeks after our trips, Mom holds onto every piece of paper she gets while we travel. I organize them for her in the scrapbook each day so she doesn't lose any of them—and she ends up with a spectacular trip souvenir that she can enjoy immediately and share with her friends as soon as she gets home.

- Send your parent postcards from the destinations you visit during your trip. My mom is in her mid-80s, and her memory is a little less sharp than it used to be. (I feel the same way about mine—and I'm in my 40s!) So sending her those postcards helps her remember our trip and prolongs the magic of the time we spent together.

Taking a Cruise

Although cruising may not top your list of vacation possibilities, it is a great option if your parent has any sort of mobility issues, because even the mega-ships are manageable—and offer plenty of things to do, too. Here are a few tips for enjoying a cruise ship with an aging parent:

- When you make your reservations, ask specifically for an accessible room that has grab bars in the shower and next to the toilet. Also request a room close to the dining and common areas. There's no reason to tire out your parents with long walks down lengthy hallways—let them save their energy for the dancing!

- Also ask in advance if the cruise company has a wheelchair you can rent for the duration of the trip and whether you can take it off the boat to go on excursions or even to look around the port. (When Mom and I cruise together, I typically take her in a wheelchair to the area around the pier, where plenty of shops and restaurants can usually be found.) Those mini-excursions may be enough for your parent, who's then ready to take a nap while you go on a more adventurous tour on your own.

- Some cruise companies offer programs specifically designed for seniors, including travelers in wheelchairs. If your company is one of them and you don't plan to rent or bring a wheelchair for the duration of the trip, be sure to ask if the company provides the wheelchair for the program or if you need to rent one for that day.

- Most cruise companies offer their own excursion programs, but I've often just hired local guides to take Mom and me around and show us the sights. This sort of arrangement works great even when passengers aren't allowed to take their boat-provided wheelchairs onshore, because you just have to walk down the gangplank and to the waiting tour taxis. Not only does hiring a local guide almost always cost less than signing on for the cruise company's program, but making your own arrangements also gives you the flexibility to call it a day when your parent gets tired. If the cruise company's regular tours are too much for your parent, private tours are a great option and they make it possible for your parent to do some organized sightseeing while being able to control when he or she returns to the ship.

- If you go on an excursion on your own while your parents stay behind on the ship, try to schedule it so that you're still available to eat meals with them. My mom and I both love eating (it's one of our favorite pastimes!), so I try not to miss a meal with her when we travel together. (Also, she can be unwilling to eat on her own—though I'm slowly helping her overcome this reluctance). I find that we have a lot of our best conversations over a great meal (and cocktail), so I definitely don't want to miss this time together if I can help it!

- If you're going to skip a meal with your parent, try to make it one that won't throw him or her off too much. When I do this, I'll typically make it breakfast and arrange for room service and a newspaper to be brought to Mom's room. That way she can enjoy a leisurely meal and morning while I'm out on an aggressive tour (one that she couldn't do with me). I try to be back before lunch so we can go to the dining room together for a proper sit-down meal.

- When you go out on an excursion on your own, make sure that your parents have something to do while you're gone, especially if you'll be away for a long time. While Mom and I were in Australia, I spent a day diving at the Great Barrier Reef. I left Mom with a menu by the hotel pool after extracting a promise from the hotel staff that they'd take great care of her while I was gone—and they did! Her poolside stay cost more than the dive trip, but we both had a fabulous time!

- Cruise ships often have a lending library where passengers can either check books out for the duration of the cruise or, in the case of "take a book, leave a book" libraries, keep them for good by exchanging them for something they've finished. Whether or not your ship has a library (ask beforehand about this), you may want to bring books (in print, electronic, or audio format—whichever works best for you) that your parent (and you!) can read during those times when he or she is relaxing and not on the go.

- Depending on the passenger demographic for a particular trip, cruise ships often offer priority boarding for those folks who need extra time moving around and getting settled, as airlines do. They don't always do this, but it doesn't hurt to ask your travel agency or cruise company if it's an option. (I always keep an eye out for anything that helps Mom and me get a jump on the crowds!)

- Get a fanny pack, purse, or other small bag for your parent to use during the trip. In addition to your room key, make sure it includes a map of the ship (I suggest reviewing this with your parent every morning), and a slip of paper with your room number on it. Yes, it's somewhat risky to have the key and room information together. But I've found that Mom is much more likely to get lost than to lose her purse. When lost, she gets incredibly frustrated and frightened—and that's something worth avoiding completely.

- Hang something fun on the outside of your door so that if your parents make it to your hallway, they'll know that they're in the right neighborhood. (Conversely, not seeing your door decoration will let them know that they're in the wrong place.) Ship hallways all look *exactly* alike, and anything that helps your parents find their way when you're not with them is a good thing.

- If you're traveling with your mother, consider bringing an extra cover-up to help her feel comfortable about sunbathing and swimming. My mom hates wearing a bathing suit (don't we all!) and balks at spending time at the pool (which is something I love to do). So I've started bringing along a fun, semi-sexy animal print cover-up for her. It's amazing—and a little scary!—to see how her attitude changes once she puts on some leopard spots!

Have Fun!

As you set out on a vacation with your parent, don't forget to plan on having fun! And don't forget that having fun starts with refining your expectations— of your parent, of yourself, and of the entire trip. If you think the trip is going to be awful before you ever walk out the door, you're setting yourself up to have a vacation that stinks. On the other hand, if you look at a shared vacation as an opportunity to relax and get to know your parent a little bit better, you'll be well on your way to having a great time. Traveling to new locales together gives both you and your parent the perfect opportunity to explore new territory—both in terms of geographical destination and in terms of your relationship with each other.

MEDICAL CONCERNS

Planning is bringing the future into the present
so that you can do something about it now.
—Alan Lakein

The only thing worse than having your own medical emergency while on vacation is standing by while someone with whom you cannot communicate works on your parent who is having a medical emergency. (Even if you speak the language of your destination, understanding advanced medical terminology can still pose challenges.) Unfortunately, I experienced this firsthand with my mom during trips to Spain, Cambodia, and China. These events taught me that the most critical part of traveling with an elderly parent is preparing for a medical emergency *before* you go on your trip. Being prepared can go a long way toward helping you handle both chronic medical conditions and issues that come up during your trip.

Vital Paperwork

Chapters 1 and 2 list questions that can help you ascertain your parent's medical condition before finalizing vacation plans. This information may play a factor in selecting a destination and influence your choice of activities. Chapter 3 details the best way to pack medications and to get them through the airport security screening more easily. I've repeated some of the information from those chapters here, so that this section can serve as a reference for older travelers with medical issues. Now let's examine other concerns that can dictate the level of emergency preparedness you'll need on your trip with your parent.

As you talk with your parent about his or her health, your primary concern should be to obtain the following information:

- A precise list of your parent's medications (both those prescribed by a doctor and over-the-counter drugs) and the dosage amount, dosage schedule, and generic name for each one. Any special handling requirements are important as well, such as whether a medicine requires refrigeration (see chapter 5) or must be administered via syringes. Carry a copy of this list with you *at all times* in the event that something happens and your parent must visit the emergency room immediately—before you can return to your hotel to retrieve documents left there. If you're traveling to a foreign country, make sure you include the medications' generic names, because the brands your parent uses may not be known there. (For example, overseas doctors will probably be unfamiliar with Tylenol but will recognize its generic names, acetaminophen and paracetamol.) Also be sure to explain why your parent is taking each medication. The medical information document I maintain for Mom, for example, includes "metformin—for type 2 diabetes."

- Contact information for all of your parent's doctors—even those for seemingly one-off medical issues. (You never know what might rear its ugly head during your vacation!) Most doctors have an emergency paging service, so be sure to get that information as well in case you need to contact a doctor during off hours.

- A list of all your parent's allergies (e.g., medicines, foods, airborne allergens). The list should also include warning signs of an aggravated condition, as well as information on what to do if your parent has a serious flare-up.

- A list of your parent's existing medical conditions (e.g., diabetes, heart murmur, anemia, lung disease). As with allergy flare-ups, be sure to include information to help you recognize and respond to any warning signs of danger.

- A copy of your parent's health-care policy (including policy numbers and contact phone numbers). Before leaving for vacation, check with the provider to find out what coverage your parent has outside the U.S. In the likely event that the policy doesn't cover overseas incidents, you may want to look into supplemental medical insurance for the trip (see chapter 4).

Although this may seem like a lot of work, once you've compiled this list the first time, keeping it up to date is fairly simple. Put all of your parent's medical information into one document and carry it with you at all times. I know I said that earlier, but it's important enough to state twice. Or even three times: *always have this document with you!*

Don't forget to bring your own prescription and doctor information with you, too. I was glad to have that information on hand when I found myself in the emergency room in Malaysia after a monkey bit me and I needed to contact my travel doctor immediately. (He confirmed my hunch that I had to get rabies shots right away, while I was still in Malaysia, and then see him upon my return to New York City.) I was "lucky" in this situation, because I was fully awake and able to manage my own care. Not everyone is so fortunate, however, so make sure your parents know where your medical information is in case you're knocked unconscious (or can't communicate for other reasons) and they need to help you get medical care.

The second most important document to carry with you during your travels is a list of hospitals in the areas you're visiting. Although the staff at your hotel can surely direct you to a nearby hospital, if an emergency occurs while you're out and about touring, you may have a hard time finding that information on the fly—for example, your cab driver might not be able to understand you. As part of my trip preparations I do my own research on hospital locations, and when I arrive at my destination, if it's in a foreign country I ask the hotel staff to translate those hospital names and addresses into the local language. I carry that list along with the hotel's contact information (which I also make sure to have in both English and the local language) so I can always get to where I need to go. When traveling with Mom, I find it better to be unnecessarily overprepared rather than be underprepared if an emergency does arise.

Last—but not least—be sure to carry a copy of everyone's passports (leaving the originals in the hotel's safe or other secure location) with you at all times, even when you're just out sightseeing for a day. Most health-care facilities will ask to see your passport (and will accept a copy of it) before they provide treatment. Although a passport isn't a universal requirement, carrying around a couple pieces of paper is only mildly inconvenient compared to not being able to provide requested documentation in the event of an emergency. In other words, better safe than sorry!

Additional Pre-Trip Preparations

In addition to putting together a medical information document for you and your parent, your preparations should include going over a number of other important questions with your parent and his or her doctor.

- Is the location you're considering currently under any health-related travel warnings or advisories from the Centers for Disease Control? Research this question well in advance of booking flights, because depending on the severity of the situation, you may wish to go elsewhere. Travel to places with such warnings can be particularly risky for older adults, whose immune systems may have weakened with age.

- Regardless of the destination overseas, consult a travel doctor to ensure that your parent's vaccines are up to date. This is critical for travel to any country, even if it has no health warnings. Something as simple as a scratch (which you can get anywhere in the world), for example, can lead to tetanus if you don't have the proper vaccines. Because some vaccines must be administered in multiple doses over an extended period of time, consult with your travel doctor at least eight to twelve weeks before departure.

- Does your parent have chronic health issues? They won't necessarily rule out travel. But you and your parent do need to understand that some comforts of home (such as elevators, private bathrooms, and air conditioning) may not be standard in hotels at your destination, particularly if you go to developing countries. (See later in this chapter for suggestions for traveling with a parent suffering from a chronic disease.)

- Is your parent sensitive to hot or cold weather or to the sun in general? How does he or she react to overexposure, and what treatment is needed in those cases? Don't forget to pack sunscreen! Regardless of the outdoor temperatures, it will come in handy if the sun is shining brightly.

- How will you manage incontinence issues? When you're out exploring, how can you get quick access to a bathroom if your parent needs it? You may want to ask your parent's doctor about medications to help with incontinence on a temporary basis. (Don't make this diagnosis on your own and pick up an over-the-counter remedy, because it can exacerbate the situation instead of making it better.)

- If you're opting for a cruise or other water plans, does your parent get seasick? What type of medical care is available on the ship if he or she becomes ill? The answer to this second question may influence your choice of cruise line: some companies have a dicey record on providing quality medical care at sea. If your parent does get seasick, opting for a larger ship on the ocean or a river cruise may be the way to go.

- Do you anticipate driving on rough roads? If so, what medicines will help with carsickness? If you're not sure what kind of roads you'll encounter while traveling, prepare for the worst by bringing antinausea medications and (if possible) making sure that there's more than one driver in your party. (As I mentioned in chapter 2, while driving the twisty road to Hana in Hawaii, I got so carsick that my mom had to take over the driving!)

- What dietary restrictions (not to mention personal preferences) should you keep in mind when selecting restaurants while on vacation?

Managing Medical Conditions during Your Trip

Even if your parents have severe medical conditions, they can still go on vacation with you. As long as you're well informed and prepare appropriately, you can manage a wide range of conditions while on the road. If you're worried about your ability to handle some things, though, consider hiring help. Several companies provide nurses who can ensure that your parents take their medicines on time and assist with other medical needs. They can either travel with you and your parents or meet you at your destination, depending on your needs (and budget). Hiring a nurse during your vacation can help you get time to relax, too—especially if you are your parent's usual caregiver.

If Your Parent Has a Chronic Disease

Unpredictability is the main factor that makes traveling with a chronic disease such a challenge. Fortunately, there are ways to mitigate its effects. It's advisable to check with your parent's doctor before planning any trip and to ask the doctor to write a detailed statement describing your parent's condition. (You'll want to have this information on hand if your parent requires medical attention during your trip.)

Once you understand what you're up against, start small for your first trip: choose a nearby location that's an easy drive from where you live and has features or attractions that interest you. Many cities have museums, for example, or noteworthy restaurants. An Internet search for "top 10 things to do in [city name]" should turn up plenty of ideas. You can also contact your destination's Chamber of Commerce or your local AAA office for more information. Posting your questions to your social media networks can help, too, because your friends are sure to have plenty of ideas!

This trip doesn't have to be full of tourist activities or visits to local attractions, though. Something as simple as an overnight stay in a hotel can be a fun mini-vacation because it's a variation from your usual routine. (For example, I've done many one-night hotel stays so I could sleep in a different bed for a night and do brunch at the hotel the next day—and have someone else cook and clean up afterward!) The holidays can be an especially good time of year for these sorts of overnight trips, because larger hotels typically have fun activities available on-site and often offer holiday-themed package deals. If you select a nearby destination and book a hotel that allows changes to the reservation, and your parent wakes up on departure day and cannot venture out of the house, then you can postpone your plans by a day in hopes that tomorrow will be better. This flexibility can also help reduce any anxiety about losing money if you need to make last-minute changes to your plans.

Whatever mini-trip you plan, your main goals should be to take it easy and to be flexible. Whether you're staying in a hotel one night or several, plan one activity for each day, followed by some relaxation time in the hotel. Mom and I frequently hang out in hotel lobbies to people-watch. We play a game in which we guess where people are going or coming from. With the assortment of people who meander by, it's pretty hilarious (and gets funnier the more cocktails we consume).

Once you and your parent try out a mini-trip or two, you may decide that you're up for travel to more far-flung destinations. Or maybe you'll decide that these small trips are the best way to balance your parent's health issues with a vacation. Either way, figuring out the perfect destination and ideal duration for your trip isn't nearly as important as spending vacation time with your parent.

If you're up for taking your parent on a vacation that requires a long-haul plane ride, consult with your parent's doctor to discuss any precautions you should take in advance or while overseas. These tips (most of which appear in other chapters as well because they are appropriate for travel with any parent) are particularly useful when taking a long-haul flight with a parent who suffers from a chronic disease:

- Select destinations reachable via a direct flight from your parent's home city. Changing planes is a pain (especially when it involves hiking through large airports), so avoid doing so whenever possible.

- Encourage your parent to lay out luggage several days before departure and to do a little bit of packing each day. Not only does this save Mom or Dad from last-minute panic and exhaustion, but it gives you both time to double- and triple-check that he or she isn't forgetting anything vital—such as medications. I also send my mom a packing checklist specific to where we're going. Without it, she has a tendency to forget what she's packed, then pulls everything out of her bags and starts all over. The checklist keeps her on track—and keeps both of us sane!

- Take advantage of any preboarding opportunities provided by the airline; ask the gate agent about this. Boarding early can help your parent avoid excessive standing and jostling, which can be exhausting for anyone.

- If you aren't flying the first trip leg with your parent, arrange ahead of time to have a friend, taxi, or car service drop him or her off at the airport so that your parent doesn't have to navigate busy roads or huge long-term parking lots.

- This suggestion is so important that it appears several times in this book: arrange in advance with the airline to have a wheelchair to take your parent to the gate. If he or she feels up to walking that day, you can cancel the wheelchair reservation at the last minute. (This hasn't happened with my mom yet, but I always give her the choice between walking or riding!)

- Pack a sleep mask and earplugs for your parent to help him or her get some sleep on the plane.

- Arrange for the hotel to have private transportation waiting for you and your parent when you land at your destination. I do this on *every* long-haul flight (whether or not Mom is traveling with me), because I don't want to hassle with getting a taxi when I'm exhausted. Even for well-seasoned travelers, dealing with taxis is challenging in *any* city—and especially in a foreign country. You and your parent are better off conserving your energy for checking out the sights, not spending it all waiting for transportation or arguing with a taxi driver.

- Travel with a tour group and let someone else do the planning, including moving you and your parent from one city to another. A cruise is another excellent option, especially if you avoid the big ships (which can be as exhausting to traverse as an airport) and instead opt for smaller ones.

- Keep activities to a minimum on your first day. Give your parents and yourself time to recover from the plane ride and the general stress of getting to your destination. Remember, you're *on vacation*. So the goal is to de-stress, not to overbook yourself. After all, you can do *that* just fine at home!

- Stay in one place for a longer period of time. Do you really need to see Rome, Florence, *and* Venice in one week? Spending time in one place and exploring the local culture can be as (or more!) rewarding than a whirlwind tour and will allow you to chill out if you need to take a break.

- Stay in a hotel rather than renting a home or apartment. You don't want to have to mess with washing the sheets or tidying up. You do that stuff at home, so let someone else do it for you while you're on vacation!

- Understand that when you return home, you and your parent may need some time to recover from the travel and the time-zone changes. So give yourselves a break and don't overschedule those first couple of days back home. Try to ease back into your routines if possible—and keep that vacation feeling going as long as you can!

Traveling with a Parent Who Has Dementia

According to the Alzheimer's Association, more than five million people are currently living with Alzheimer's disease, and the number is estimated to *triple* by 2050. Alzheimer's disease accounts for up to 70% of cases of dementia; the rest are caused by Parkinson's disease and various other disorders. With such a significant segment of the senior population being affected by dementia, you may find one of your own family members stricken with it, so it's good to understand what options exist for traveling with a parent who has this condition.

It is possible to travel with someone who has dementia, but whether or not that's a good idea for you and your parent depends a great deal on his or her ability to handle change—something that is often difficult for those suffering from dementia. After all, travel is all about experiencing change: new locations, new foods, new experiences. All of that change may be too overwhelming for a parent who is in the advanced stages of dementia.

Making Plans and Taking Precautions

Before making travel plans, first consult with your parent's doctor about your parent's ability to handle a trip. Ask for suggestions for managing any behavioral changes that could occur during your travels, and ask if an anti-anxiety medication would be useful during the trip—for your parent, of course, not for you!

Because changes in environment can trigger wandering in dementia patients, consider equipping your parent with a GPS-based tracking device. (Several companies offer this service specifically for people with dementia. Your parent's doctor should be able to give you a recommendation; you can also find information through an Internet search.) At a minimum, your parent should have identification on his or her person (such as a medical alert bracelet that isn't easily removed or lost) that will allow authorities to contact you if they find your parent wandering alone.

Even if your parent has a tracking device or ID, however, *never* leave him or her alone. Bring your parent with you (even when you visit a restroom), because it's not uncommon for people suffering from dementia to forget that they are waiting for someone and go off on their own.

Because change can be unsettling to people with dementia, many experts recommend traveling to destinations that were already familiar to your parent before the onset of dementia. That isn't always possible, however, and you may end up taking a trip to a new location. In that case, it's important to get your parent back on a routine (preferably similar to the one he or she has at home) as quickly as possible when you arrive. Of course, before making any firm plans to travel together, be sure to discuss the impending trip with your parent and get a sense of how he or she feels about it. If merely talking about a trip makes your parent severely anxious, that may be a sign that it's best to leave your parent at home. But if he or she seems excited about a new adventure, then go for it!

Looking Out for Your Parent

If possible, bring along at least one other able adult (such as another family member, a friend, or a caregiver) to ensure that your parent is never left alone. If you and your parent are traveling with others, your trip planning should include a comprehensive discussion of everyone's roles and responsibilities. Topics to cover include:

- Who will help Mom or Dad pack? Packing can be particularly stressful for a parent who's struggling to remember what to bring. And it doesn't help *your* stress level, either, to arrive at your destination only to discover that your parent forgot a critical item. So give your parent some much-needed help with this task.

- Who will make sure that your parent takes his or her medications at the correct times each day? Even though my mom has had the same pill regimen for more than 15 years, changes in her daily routine throw her off her schedule, and she cannot remember to take her medicine when she's on the road. This effect is even stronger with people who have dementia, so do not expect them to manage medications on their own.

- Who will be on "parent duty" at the airport? An airport's crowds and activity can make it a particularly frightening place to someone with dementia. While you're in the airport, someone should stay by your parent's side *at all times*—even if another member of your party is struggling with luggage, trying to corral young children, or dealing with one of the many things that can go wrong at the airport.

- When you reach your destination, who will help your parent unpack and establish routines? A conversation on this topic should also include determining which routines are most important for your parent.

- If Mom or Dad needs a break or decides not to venture out of the hotel room, who will stay with him or her?

- If you're out sightseeing and your parent becomes agitated and needs to return to the hotel quickly, who will go with him or her, and how will they get there?

Lodging Options

When traveling with a parent who has dementia, staying in separate rooms is *not* recommended; instead, consider upgrading to a suite or condo with two rooms so you can have some privacy yet still hear if a problem arises. As much as possible, any routines your parent has at home (sleeping with the bathroom light on, etc.) should be duplicated in your hotel room. Because a change in venue can trigger night walking in some people with dementia, your parent should sleep in the room farthest from the door to make it more difficult for him or her to leave undetected. Leaning a chair against the door to the hallway can also dissuade your parent from leaving the room, because even if he or she can unlock and open the door, the chair obstacle may be too difficult to negotiate.

Also consider getting a hotel room or suite with a kitchen so you can prepare foods you know your parent enjoys. Remember that maintaining a routine includes sticking to familiar foods and dining times, so don't expect your parent to try new foods while you're on vacation. And when you're out sightseeing, pack some of your parent's favorite foods in case he or she doesn't want anything on the restaurant menu.

Transit Tips

Whether you're driving or flying, try to travel during the time of day when your parent is at his or her best. If this means flying during peak times, you may have to pay for higher airfares. But creating the most comfortable environment for your parent (and therefore for you, too!) should be your top priority, so treat that extra cost as a necessary expense in your trip budget. And regardless of your mode of travel, keep your parent apprised of your trip progress; knowing when the end of the journey is near will help him or her stay calm and feel less anxious.

If you're driving to your destination, build time into your schedule to stop and stretch every couple of hours. A bit of exercise and fresh air can dissipate any growing anxiety about being cooped up and help keep everyone's stress levels to a minimum.

If you're flying to your destination, try to book a direct flight; if that's not possible, avoid tight connections, because rushing from one gate to another can trigger anxiety in your parent (heck, it triggers anxiety in me, too!).

Even seasoned travelers find airports to be noisy, chaotic places, and they're even worse for someone suffering from dementia—and especially when that person has to hurry.

Navigating an airport is definitely a situation in which a second able adult is needed: someone must be focused on your parent *at all times*. Yes, you'll be physically close to Mom or Dad, but chances are you'll be checking luggage, arranging a wheelchair, managing carry-ons, and tending to myriad other tasks before you even start walking to the security screening area. Bringing along an additional adult traveling companion or hiring a caregiver can ensure that your parent gets the attention he or she needs and doesn't wander off alone.

Keep in mind these additional recommendations when flying:

- When booking your reservations, make sure that you are seated right next to your parent (*no exceptions!*).

- Arrive at the airport extra early to allow plenty of time to get through security. Rushing to catch a flight will put you (and everyone traveling with you—especially a parent who is already anxious) on edge. As you're approaching the security screening area, inform the TSA agents that your parent has dementia and may need extra time and help getting through the checkpoint.

- Because being overtired can trigger dementia symptoms, book wheelchair assistance with your airline. As you go through security, a wheelchair will give your parent a place to sit while you're rounding up all your belongings.

- If you belong to the airline's frequent flyer program, consider purchasing day passes to that company's airport lounge so you and your parent have a quiet place to wait for your flight.

- When boarding the plane, inform the flight attendants that you are traveling with a parent who has dementia. If anything happens to you, they can pass this information along to a medical crew if necessary.

Activities at Your Destination

One key to a successful vacation with a parent who has dementia is getting him or her back into a routine as quickly as possible once you arrive at your destination. Keeping to regular times for waking up and going to bed can be helpful, particularly with people who suffer from sundowning or other sleep issues associated with dementia.

When scheduling activities, try to plan them for the time of day when your parent functions best. Pushing people with dementia too hard can have disastrous results, so be selective in your choice of activity and schedule plenty of supervised downtime so your parent can relax. Also build in extra time for meals, bathing, and dressing. (It's a good idea to add extra time for *everything*. Rushing can severely stress your parent and cause dementia symptoms to worsen.)

Don't forget to involve your parent in *your* regular activities, too. Remember, routines can help people with dementia enjoy themselves. So bring your parent along on your morning walk or coffee run (and make sure you follow the same route each time).

Whether it's advisable to travel with a parent who has dementia depends on his or her condition. Before organizing a big trip, you may want to test the waters by going somewhere local first. Wherever you go (and for whatever duration), providing your parent with constant, calming companionship can help ensure a successful trip. To reiterate, I discourage you from trying to do this on your own, because traveling safely with a person who has dementia requires at least two able adults. I *strongly* recommend enlisting a family member or hiring a caregiver to go on vacation with you.

Traveling with a Parent on Dialysis

You may wonder whether your parent can travel if he or she requires regular dialysis treatments. The good news? With a little bit of extra planning, it's quite possible for your parent to safely travel and continue treatments while on vacation. As usual, before booking a trip, confirm with your parent's doctor that he or she is healthy enough for travel. Once the doctor gives the okay for a trip, it's time to start making plans!

Many dialysis centers offer assistance with finding treatment facilities in other parts of the world. You can also ask your parent's doctor for recommendations or research the Internet for information. As long as you're traveling to a fairly well-developed area, you're likely to find a nearby facility. And if you're considering taking a cruise, your arrangements might be even easier: there are companies that specialize in providing hemodialysis care on cruise ships.

The biggest challenge (as you probably know from experiences with your parent's own local facility) is getting a slot for treatment in a dialysis center; this can be particularly difficult at popular vacation spots. Start your planning at least six weeks before your trip (even longer if you're traveling over the holidays or during other peak travel periods), and be prepared to contact several places until you find one that works for your parent. You may even want to hold off on booking flights until you've found a place with availability that meets your time and place criteria.

As soon as you arrive at your destination, reconfirm your appointment times with the dialysis center. If you like, you can also schedule a preappointment visit to the center. Don't show up there unannounced, though— always book this in advance.

Have your parent's primary dialysis center send the required medical forms to the transient center well ahead of your arrival to allow plenty of time for a review before your parent shows up for treatment. (Plan on hand-carrying a copy of all your records with you as well.) To accommodate a transient patient, centers typically require the following information:

- medical history and recent physical exam reports
- recent lab results, EKG, and chest X-ray
- dialysis prescription
- records of three to five recent treatments

- dialysis access type

- description of special needs or dialysis requirements

- insurance information

- all prescription medications (including any that must be given during dialysis)

- contact information for all your parent's doctors and your parent's at-home dialysis center

Even if a transient center does not specifically ask for all this information, it's wise to carry it with you anyway in case your parent has an issue while on the road. Although the dialysis center you visit while on vacation can assist your parent if he or she becomes ill, make sure you also always carry a list of local hospitals in case your parent needs emergency care.

If your parent does home hemodialysis, you, your parent, and his or her current dialysis care team should discuss the advisability of continuing home dialysis while on the road. It's probably easier to do in-center treatment while on vacation than to haul all the equipment with you while traveling. If your parent opts for home dialysis, however, make sure you know the location of the closest center in case any problems arise. When you reach your destination, contact that center to let them know you're in the area and confirm their emergency procedures.

Keep in mind that Medicare and your parent's secondary insurance might not cover dialysis (including any doctor's fees while at the transient center) while you're on the road. Confirm coverage with your parent's insurance carriers prior to departure, so you know what to expect.

Traveling with a Diabetic Parent

If your parent is diabetic, always carry juice boxes, hard candy, or other snacks with you in the event that travel delays make it difficult to keep to a meal schedule and your parent's blood sugar drops unexpectedly. (And even if your parent is not diabetic, it's still a good idea to have snacks handy at all times.) I also highly recommend purchasing a to-go meal shortly before boarding the plane so your parent will be sure to have something that meets his or her dietary needs. Even if you're in first class (where meals are provided) or if your flight has food for sale, pick up something before you board, in case you encounter any surprises. For example, I've been on flights that have run out of food because the galleys weren't stocked before takeoff. Don't forget to carry portable glucose testers with you at all times so you can quickly check your parent's blood sugar and take counteractive measures if it drops.

Travel Insurance

I've discussed travel insurance in detail elsewhere (see chapter 4). Not all travelers need it, but when traveling with a parent who has a serious medical condition, I highly recommend purchasing some that allows for last-minute trip cancellation. If you have this insurance and need to cancel your trip for health-related issues (or other reasons), you may be able to get most of your money back. Search the Internet for "travel insurance" or check out a travel insurance aggregation site.

After the Vacation

After you return from vacation with a parent who suffers from a serious medical condition and has required a lot of your time and attention, a little mini-vacation for yourself seems highly in order. As part of your trip planning, schedule at least one day of post-trip downtime on your own (maybe a spa day?) before returning to work so you can rest and recharge. You've earned it!

STAYING SAFE BEFORE, DURING, AND AFTER YOUR VACATION

Safety is something that happens between your ears,
not something you hold in your hands.
—Jeff Cooper

I consider myself to be a fairly savvy traveler who pays attention to her sur-roundings and thinks about safety while traveling. When I'm with Mom, I focus even more on security issues, because thieves and scammers around the world often target older tourists. By no means do I think of the world as a danger zone. Quite the opposite, actually: the vast majority of people Mom and I have met have been welcoming, accommodating, and helpful (particularly when we're outside the U.S.). That said, I still take certain pre-cautions to ensure that we'll both have a great time and return home in one piece—and with all our belongings intact!

Pre-Vacation Precautions

Selecting a Destination

As I mentioned in chapter 2, one of your first tasks when planning a trip should be to check the Centers for Disease Control website (www.cdc.gov) for information about any destinations you're considering. The CDC issues three levels of travel health notices, depending on the preventability and severity of the disease in question. You could still consider travel to an area with a measles outbreak, for example, if you and your parent have the required vaccines and are in good health. In the case of a level 3 warning (for an ebola outbreak, for example), though, you should avoid that place entirely.

Another great tool for evaluating the safety of certain areas is the travel website for the U.S. Department of State (www.travel.state.gov), which issues travel warnings and travel alerts for countries whose current situations may be dangerous to American travelers. If a country is under a travel warning, you should seriously consider going elsewhere, because it indicates something major such as ongoing violence, severe government unrest, or frequent terrorist attacks. A travel alert, on the other hand, is typically issued for a short period of time; situations that warrant an alert include a contentious election with potentially violent demonstrations, a strike, a temporary health crisis that is expected to be contained, an impending weather situation (such as a hurricane), or a terrorist threat level raised in response to a particular event or chatter from the police.

Be sure to look at the State Department's main website, too. It has a plethora of travel information beyond travel warnings and alerts. It's a great place to find analyses of a country's politics, crime rate, and weather (to name a few types of data) and a useful site to review when planning any international travel, regardless of your destination.

Before finalizing my choice of location, I also do a general Internet search about it and check TripAdvisor (or other travel sites with reviews or discussion forums) for advice from travelers who have visited that area. In particular, I look for information about how safe it is to venture out at night, about the hotel's security, and about the area around the hotel. In short, I want data that tells me what to expect when I arrive. When I'm traveling by myself, I'm a bit less rigorous in this research. But when I'm traveling with Mom, I have to make sure that we avoid sketchy areas. They make Mom uncomfortable (and I don't say that lightly—they truly freak her out!), which means it's impossible for her to relax. And if she's not enjoying herself at a destination, what's the point in going on vacation there?

Choosing a Tour Operator

In 2005, I was booked on a hiking tour of the Inca Trail to Machu Picchu, Peru, but the week before I was due to get on the plane out of New York, I realized that the outfit I'd hired to pick me up at the Lima airport and take me to Cusco (the city at the start of the trail) had scammed me. How did I know? The company's phone number suddenly stopped working, and no one would return my e-mails. In other words, the company basically disappeared.

I was determined to hike that trail, though. So I decided to fly to Peru as planned. Nervous about what I would find (or not find) when I landed in Lima, I lined up an alternate vendor to take me to Cusco if indeed my suspicions about the original vendor were correct. Alas, I didn't get a chance to try either my original plan or my backup plan: two days before my departure, my father passed away unexpectedly, and I canceled my entire trip.

Needless to say, this little fiasco turned out to be a valuable learning experience for me. Here's my hard-earned advice: *before forking over any money to tour operators or other travel providers, check them out as thoroughly as you can.*

As I mentioned in chapter 5, the Better Business Bureau is a great place to start your research on U.S.-based companies. Take a look at independent review sites (such as TripAdvisor) and discussion boards (such as Lonely Planet's Thorn Tree forum). Also check directly with the United States Tour Operators Association (USTOA), the National Tour Association (NTA), or the American Society of Travel Agents (ASTA) to see if any of them has vetted your tour company. (Note, however, that those organizations include only companies in North America.) And if you're hiring a tour operator to take you on a potentially risky excursion (such as parasailing or scuba diving), it's even more important to make sure it's a legitimate operation with all the required qualifications before you sign up for anything.

In lieu of getting references from the tour operator, I usually ask my connections on various social media platforms (LinkedIn, Facebook, etc.) for recommendations. I did call the references provided by the operator in Peru and received glowing comments from them, but when the tour company disappeared, the references did too. In the wake of that disaster, I now prefer the experience of friends (or friends of friends) over the comments of whomever the operator offers up. Even when you're comfortable with a particular tour company, it's still a good idea to play it safe and double-check all of the hotel rooms, flights, and other arrangements yourself once the company has sent you confirmation of your bookings. (I learned this lesson, too, the hard way after a travel agent kept all the money I had paid it and never booked my cruise!) And before booking anything, check your credit card company's fraud protection plan to see if you're eligible for any refunds in the event of a problem.

One final warning: if a tour is cheap, there's probably a reason for that low price. Run—don't walk—away from that operator and find someone else!

Researching Travel Insurance

Travel medical insurance (see chapter 4) can save the day (and your wallet!) if you or your parent get sick or injured during a vacation abroad. But what about all the stuff you bring with you? And how do you protect yourself from a tour operator that goes out of business, doesn't deliver on your contract, or pulls a disappearing act (like my Peruvian friends)? Travel insurance (the nonmedical kind) can give you peace of mind about your finances—though you'll still have to deal with the stress of having a problem with your vacation!

There is a wide range of travel insurance options out there, and choosing the right ones for you can be quite challenging (especially because there is *a lot* of fine print to read). So don't save this research for the last couple of weeks immediately before your trip. You'll have enough other stuff to worry about during that period (particularly if you don't live near your parent and are trying to help him or her get prepared for your vacation together), and wading through the various contracts' details can take some time. It's best to do this research during the early stages of your vacation planning, not only so you have enough time to weigh all of your options carefully, but also so you're covered if something happens right before your trip.

When evaluating insurance options, keep in mind that the most expensive policy isn't always the best policy. Before you purchase any insurance, *read the fine print* and understand exactly what is, and is not, covered. Here are a few of the coverage categories usually found in travel insurance policies:

- **Cancellation or operator insolvency.** Travel insurance policies typically require you to list the costs (which you must be able to prove with receipts in the event of a problem) of your tour or travel arrangements, including any add-ons. Keep in mind that the higher a trip's cost, the higher a premium you'll pay. You'll want to ask these questions:

  - What happens if a company goes bankrupt (or simply disappears)?

  - What is the payout policy if you and your parent get sick before departure and you need to cancel the trip?

  - What happens if one of you is sick and the other isn't but does not want to take the trip alone? (For example, some policies may reimburse your parent's trip expenses if he or she gets sick and has to stay home, but may not offer you a simultaneous reimbursement if you're not sick but want to stay behind with your parent.)

- **Travel delays.** In this age of overbooked planes and overcrowded skies, flight delays and cancellations have become increasingly common, with effects that can ripple throughout the rest of your vacation. For example, a delayed flight may cause you to miss a reserved hotel night, for which you might be charged even if you're not there. Or if you've booked a cruise and miss the boat's departure, you may have to purchase a new plane ticket in order to meet the ship at a later port of call. In both of these situations, a travel delay policy can help you avoid those extra costs. Keep in mind, though, that the provisions of such a policy typically don't kick in until after you experience a 24-hour delay (and not after just a few hours of pain and suffering in an airport).

- **Lost, stolen, or delayed luggage.** Having luggage problems is always my greatest fear when traveling, mostly because I *hate* shopping—and having to replace my possessions because my luggage has wandered off in a foreign country or gotten lost on the way is, to me, an awful way to start a vacation. Check your airline's luggage policy first so you know at what point your independent insurance policy takes effect. When researching a policy that covers luggage issues, clarify what happens if your luggage is stolen while you're en route to your hotel (e.g., taken from the backseat or even the trunk of a rental car while you stop for a quick bite to eat).

- **Personal liability.** This is the big kahuna of the travel insurance world. This policy provides coverage in the event someone sues you for causing him or her to suffer a personal injury. Possible scenarios include someone tripping over your power cord while you're checking e-mail at a coffee shop, or if you're shopping and accidentally knock over an item that injures another customer. Because personal liability situations are so varied—and so unpredictable—I typically purchase fairly substantial coverage (in the range of several million dollars) to make sure I have enough to cover someone's medical bills, lost wages, and other costs if he or she successfully sues me over something that happens during my trip.

- **Car rental.** Don't assume that your current car insurance or even your general travel insurance will cover you when you rent a car. To get coverage for this situation, you usually need to arrange it directly with the car rental company. Check this out before your trip so you know in advance what insurance you'll need—and so you have plenty of time to go through all the complicated legalese. I travel often and *still* find car rental insurance confusing everywhere I go (and especially in a foreign country). Some credit card companies offer coverage when you use their cards to rent a car, so be sure to check on that, too. Finally, keep in mind that personal liability coverage from a travel policy usually won't cover you if you're in a car accident, so be sure to look into getting a policy that fills that gap.

To reiterate: *always read (and understand!) the fine print on every insurance policy.* This goes for all trip-related policies from airlines, car rental companies, and travel insurance companies. But it's also true for everyday policies, such as homeowners insurance and auto insurance, because sometimes those may offer you some coverage when you travel, and before you hit the road you need to know exactly what coverage you have (or don't have). If you're spending a lot of money on a trip or if you're going with an aging parent, I highly recommend getting travel-specific insurance, because you never know when something might happen that leads to a trip cancellation. And if you have insurance, your costs will be reimbursed, giving you the money you need to reschedule your trip for another time.

Right Before Departure

Some tasks—such as researching travel insurance and making plane and hotel reservations—need to be done months before your trip. Many of the tasks that focus on personal security measures, however, are best taken care of during the one or two weeks before departure.

Getting Your Equipment Ready to Travel

- If you plan to take a laptop or other computer equipment on your trip, make sure it's updated with the latest and greatest security software. If your parent is bringing a computer, be sure to check it as well.

- If you haven't already password-protected your smartphone, do so. (This is particularly critical while traveling, though it's something you should seriously consider doing when you're at home, too.) Like most people, you probably keep all of your passwords and other personal information on your smartphone, so use a password to avoid unwanted access to that data. (I don't want strangers to access my personal info—and I also don't want anyone calling Mom from my phone!)

Packing

- Clean out your purse and wallet, leaving behind unnecessary items such as your checkbook, address books, or membership IDs. If your bag is stolen, you don't want a thief identifying you (and, consequently, the address of your empty house) from your Sam's Club membership card!

- Do, however, put your name, cell phone number, and e-mail address (but not your home address) on the inside of your bag in case the identification tags on the outside get torn off.

- Leave your gold (including any wedding ring more ornate than a simple band) and other fancy jewelry at home, particularly if you are going to a place where those will make you a target for thieves. (These places include many less developed countries, but high-tourism areas in more affluent locales can also be risky.) As a tourist, you'll still stand out in the crowd, but would-be thieves will be more likely to assume that you don't have anything of value on you if they don't see flashy jewelry.

Gathering Important Documents

- As mentioned in chapter 5, make copies or take pictures of important documents for both you and your parent. These include credit cards (make sure you have the companies' emergency phone numbers, too), travel documents (e.g., flight and hotel confirmations), prescriptions, and passports.

- E-mail a copy of the documents to yourself (or save them in the cloud), keep one copy with you, and e-mail one copy to a trusted friend back home. In the event your wallet or purse is stolen or lost during your trip, having these copies will make it *a lot* easier for you to get replacement documents quickly (particularly a passport) and cancel any cards before a burglar tests the upper end of your credit limit.

- If you e-mail those copies to anyone or store them on your smartphone, password protection for that device is even more critical!

Preparing (and Protecting) Your Home

- If you're employing a house sitter or dog walker while you're away, lock up your valuables and sensitive documents, including bank statements, credit card bills, and other forms that contain your personal information.

- Put holds on mail and newspaper deliveries for both you and your parent, and ask neighbors to keep an eye on your home and your parent's home.

- Finally, as much as you'd like to tell everyone about your upcoming travels (particularly if you're heading to a fabulous locale!), resist the urge to post about it on Facebook. I know, I know—that's asking a lot! But because Facebook (and other social media sites) can't guarantee your privacy, and because posts often get shared far beyond their intended recipients (to friends of friends, then to *their* friends, whom you don't know), you're better off keeping quiet. By posting about your trip, you're basically telling the world, "I'll be out of town on *these exact dates*"—a statement that some unscrupulous characters might interpret as an invitation to pay your house (and your possessions) a visit during your absence. I love connecting with friends through social media, and I love to talk about my travels, so I struggle myself with keeping mum about upcoming trips. But it's in my best interests in the long run to do so—and I encourage you to follow suit. And remember, you can post about your trip all you like, with plenty of photos, after you get home!

Informing the U.S. Consulate of Your Travel Plans

The Smart Traveler Enrollment Program (STEP) is a great free program provided by the U.S. Department of State. Before you travel, simply create an account on the STEP website (www.step.state.gov) and provide your dates of travel, your destination, and some personal information (such as an emergency contact who is not traveling with you). Once enrolled, you'll receive travel warnings and advisories about your destination. You'll also be on file with the U.S. embassy or consulate there, making it much easier for its staff to help you in an emergency. They can provide assistance with serious medical or financial difficulties, put you in contact with local doctors and lawyers, and even provide private loans in emergency situations.

When you travel, bring with you the contact information (especially the address and phone number) for the nearest U.S. consulate or embassy in each area you'll be visiting. In the event of a problem while traveling, you'll be glad to have this information handy so you won't need to hunt it down while you're in the middle of a crisis. You'll also need it if you lose your passport and have to go to the consulate or embassy for a replacement (more on that later in this chapter).

While on Vacation

I know that when I'm tired and cranky, I'm not paying attention to my sur-roundings, nor are my decision-making abilities at their best. Therefore, well before Mom and I start our trip, I typically arrange for our hotel at our destination to have a car waiting for us at the airport when we arrive. It's almost a magical experience to come out of customs and see someone hold-ing a sign with our names on it! Having a prearranged private car ride to the hotel means I don't have to haggle over a fare or deal with taxi drivers who may or may not speak English.

After living in New York City for many years and traveling all over the world, I've taken more than my fair share of taxi rides. Based on that expe-rience, I know that taxi drivers aren't always totally honest about their fares—and that's especially true when they know they've got a tourist in the car. More times than not, when I've taken a taxi abroad my driver has taken the long way around when going from point A to point B. Most of the time, I haven't minded, because I consider these rides opportunities to see a bit more of the surrounding area. But after I've had a long plane flight (and have possibly spent a lot of time in lines at baggage claim, customs, and immigration), I'm not in the mood for sightseeing. At that point, I want a car to get me to the hotel as fast as possible so I can shower and lie down for a few minutes before going out to explore. These arrangements help Mom and me make an easier transition to our new surroundings—and they may do the same for you and your parent.

Once you're rested, keep these additional safety precautions in mind as you head out on your excursions.

Protecting Your Computer

- Be wary of using public computers in Internet cafes, hotels, etc., because they are prime spots for someone to hack into your per-sonal accounts. If you must use a public computer, though, never autosave information, and always make sure you fully close applications before walking away. (To be on the safe side, delete your search history and cookies, too.) Avoid doing any sort of banking activities from public computers.

- While you travel, use only secure wireless networks—not the free Wi-Fi often available in Internet cafes and other public locations—and turn off the autoconnect feature (typically found in your phone's settings) that makes your phone automatically look for and join Wi-Fi networks.

Locking Up Your Valuables

- When you're out touring for the day, lock up your passport and other important documents in your hotel's safe and take copies of them with you. This way, you still have easy access to the information if you need it (for example, if a medical emergency arises), but you don't risk losing the originals.

- Lock up prescriptions in the hotel safe as well to prevent their theft. You never know what may be valuable on the black market in the country you're visiting. And missing a dose or two of medication could be catastrophic for your parent.

Using Credit Cards Instead of Debit Cards

- Using a debit card overseas can be dangerous: if your account is hacked and a thief steals all your money, you might not know about this for days (or even weeks). Adding insult to injury, after you prove you were hacked it can still take weeks for your bank to put the money back in your account!

- Because of these risks, I always have Mom leave her debit card at home. But if you or your parent are set on taking a debit card on your vacation, financial experts recommend using it only as a credit card (and not as a debit card) so that no one you meet can directly access the funds in your account. You may also want to ask your bank if it offers prepaid debit cards or even traveler's checks, both of which are better options than using your regular debit card (and possibly having your PIN stolen).

- If you have multiple credit cards, contact each provider to determine who has the lowest fees for foreign transactions. These fees can add up *very* quickly, so know before you go.

Managing Cash

- Although credit cards are used in almost every country, it is up to each merchant whether to accept credit, so you should plan on bringing cash with you. I've found that "big" merchants, such as hotels and car rental agencies, usually require credit cards (at least for a deposit). But many smaller merchants either do not take credit or strongly prefer cash (so much so that they might offer you a lower price if you pay in cash). Remember, credit card companies charge fees, and smaller merchants are most likely to pass those costs on to the consumer.

- Before leaving for a trip abroad, I like to get some cash in the local currency of my destination, in case there's any sort of delay and I need to buy food (or something else) for Mom and me shortly after arrival. That's not always possible, though, so you may have to wait until you reach your destination before you can change money. Avoid this situation if you can, because not only are you traveling without local currency, but when you change your money at your destination you mark yourself both as a tourist and as a possible target. For example, I couldn't get Cambodian riel before I left the U.S. (not even at JFK International Airport). After we exchanged our money at the airport in Phnom Penh, Mom and I felt lots of eyes watching us, which made us both nervous!

- I try to avoid using ATMs on the road, because thieves are getting better and better at installing fake ATMs or card skimmers designed to register someone's PIN. To be fully prepared in the event that I do need to withdraw cash during my trip, though, prior to departure I ask my bank for a list of secure ATM machines in the area I'm visiting. If I need cash in an area I'm unfamiliar with (such as an area where I'm sightseeing for the day), I'll use only ATMs associated with large banks or hotel chains (although even these can be compromised, so check them carefully). When using any ATM, be sure to hide the keypad with your hand as you enter your PIN in case someone (or a camera) is watching you. There are also some great smartphone apps that can help you find ATMs when you're abroad. (I suggest that you research and download those before your trip, though, so you can avoid high data-usage fees overseas.)

- Another alternative to withdrawing cash from ATMs while traveling is to bring traveler's checks. Before opting for this route, however, check the fees for buying and using the traveler's checks, and look into the ready availability of places where you can cash the checks. It may be cheaper (and easier) to merely withdraw money from an ATM.

- One more option for obtaining cash abroad: if you're staying at a large hotel, inquire if the staff can give you local currency and add the transaction to your room bill.

- As you probably know all too well, fees for pulling from nonaffili-ated banks can be quite expensive, so it's well worth comparing your options before you go.

- One final (but critical) piece of advice: don't carry all of your cash with you when you go out. Always leave some back in the room in case your purse or wallet is stolen or lost. Keep in mind, too, that flashing a big wad of cash when you're out can make you a more likely target for thieves.

Managing Credit Cards

- Overseas, Visa and MasterCard are more readily accepted, particularly by smaller merchants, than other credit cards, such as American Express (which charges higher fees to merchants) and Discover (which is largely unknown outside the U.S.). Be sure to bring a card that's widely available at your destination and that has reasonable fees for foreign transactions.

- Inform your credit card companies of your travel itinerary. This is particularly important if you don't travel a great deal, because an unusual charge on your card may cause the company to assume that someone has stolen your card number—and then disable your card. It can be annoying and inconvenient when this happens (especially if you are in the middle of a purchase!), but with all the fraud that goes on I can understand why the companies take this course of action.

- If you're vacationing overseas, check before you leave home if your credit card issuer charges foreign transaction fees for purchases made in a foreign country. These fees can be quite high and completely blow your budget if you're not careful. Many companies (such as American Express) do not charge these fees on some of their credit cards, so be sure to research your options before heading out on the road.

- Get (and keep) receipts for *all* of your purchases. When traveling I always bring an empty envelope with me, and each night I dump that day's receipts in there. After my trip, when I check my credit card statements at home, I have all my receipts in one place (and don't have to dig through all my bags to find them). A little bit of organization up front makes for a quick review of your credit card charges later.

- Don't carry all of your credit cards with you when you visit tourist sites. Leave one card in the hotel safe, in case your purse or wallet is stolen or lost while you're out. The speed and ease with which you can quickly get a replacement card depends a lot on where you are, so make sure you have a backup safely stowed in the hotel safe in your room.

Keeping Your Wallet Secure

- We've probably all made fun of someone wearing a fanny pack, because those things scream "tourist" like nobody's business. As unfashionable as they are, though, they succeed admirably at their function of keeping your belongings in front of you, where you can see them at all times. Fortunately, there are plenty of more fashionable (yet just as utilitarian) alternatives out there.

- Many travelers swear by money belts that hang inside your pants leg or strap around your waist. They're pretty secure because they're completely hidden from view and are difficult to steal without your notice. (If you use one of these, though, make sure you get one made of a waterproof material that's easily wiped clean so it doesn't start to smell after a long sweaty day of exploring!) Another option is to keep your wallet in an inside pocket of your jacket or, if it has a button closure, a front pants pocket.

- If you're using your pocket, a fanny pack, or any other storage that's visible or not worn next to your skin, be especially wary of anyone who comes up close to you. When Mom and I were in Italy, for example, beggars would try to hand us a baby to distract us while their hands explored Mom's fanny pack (fortunately, they were unsuccessful in their attempts to rob us). It can be quite unnerving to push back against someone who's trying to put something in your hands, but don't be tricked into holding anything for a stranger.

- Try to keep your belongings in front of you at all times. Don't hang your purse on the back of the chair, for example—try to bring a bag that's small enough to sit on the table in front of you (not at your feet). And meanwhile, if you're mugged, hand over your wallet or other items (more reason to leave your wedding ring at home). Ending up in the hospital would ruin the best of plans—including the rest of your vacation. And the items you lose are just *things*: if you've got insurance, you can replace them.

Getting Around Town

- Before heading out on your first excursion, take a hotel business card from the concierge. (If the hotel address isn't already listed in the local language, ask the concierge to print it on the card.) There's nothing better than knowing that after a long day of travel, you'll be able to use it to ask for directions if you get lost or show it to a taxi driver so he or she can take you to where you're staying. Even if you don't speak the local language, all you have to do is point to the card.

- Ask the hotel concierge about the safest times to use public transportation. You never know when you or your loved one will need to take a break and return to the hotel—and cabs aren't always easy to flag down. The more informed you are about your transportation options, the easier it will be for you and your parent to relax.

- Motor scooters can be a lot of fun and usually aren't expensive to rent, but I recommend avoiding them entirely when you're traveling abroad. They are pretty dangerous (in Thailand, for example, 38 people die *each day* because of motor scooter accidents!), so you're better off choosing a different mode of transportation. And keep in mind that many travel insurance policies don't cover accidents on motor scooters.

Dealing with Security Problems during Your Trip

- Unfortunately, if your passport is lost or stolen while you're on vacation overseas, you must replace it before attempting to return to the United States. This is where doing your homework will pay off, because you'll need to go to the nearest U.S. embassy or consulate and report that your passport has been lost or stolen. (Most U.S. embassies and consulates have regular visiting hours only on weekdays, so if you lose your passport on a weekend, you'll likely be stuck at least until the next weekday.) You'll need to bring the following documents with you when you apply for a passport replacement:

- One passport photo

- Other identification (such as a driver's license)

- Evidence of U.S. citizenship (such as a photocopy of your missing passport)

- Your travel itinerary (including airline and train tickets)

- If applicable and available, a police report about your missing passport

• If you're overseas and are in a life-or-death situation or have been the victim of a serious crime, contact the nearest U.S. embassy or consulate as soon as possible. In addition to serving as diplomatic outposts, embassies and consulates also exist to assist their countries' citizens. They usually have staff available around the clock to handle emergencies, so reach out to them at any hour.

When You're Back Home

Your travels may be over (for now!), but you still have one more important trip-related task to complete: a thorough review of your credit card statements to verify that they show only your actual charges. Don't wait until your monthly statement arrives to do this, because delaying may give thieves a lot of time to spend your money. Instead, check your online records, which often show transactions mere minutes after they're made, for suspicious charges. And in case someone snagged your credit card information and waited a few days or weeks before selling it, keep checking your online statements for several weeks after your return.

Final Thoughts

When you're traveling, your top priority is to experience another place and culture. And when you're traveling with your parent, your top priority is to share quality time as you explore another place and culture together. The vast majority of people in the world are kind and generous, but there are some whose actions could ruin your vacation—or worse. Fortunately, taking a few simple precautions can help you and your parent have the peace of mind you need to feel safe while traveling. Then instead of spending all of your precious vacation time worrying, you can spend it enjoying each other's company and your amazing adventures together!

EASING BACK INTO EVERYDAY LIFE

Why do you go away? So that you can come back.
—Terry Pratchett

One great thing about travel is that it comes in so many different flavors. Trips can vary by duration, destination, types of activities—if you can name it, it's probably possible. One less-than-great thing about vacation, though, is that it must come to an end. (If it didn't, it would be "regular life" and not "vacation"!) And many people—including Mom and me—have a tough time getting back in the swing of things back home after a trip.

Think about it: during your vacation, you might have been sleeping late, eating rich foods (and probably too much of them, too!), drinking way more than usual, and pretty much doing whatever you want. No wonder you experience sheer terror the first morning the alarm goes off when you're home from vacation! As crazy as it sounds, though, going back to work and getting back into other routines can help stave off post-trip depression by giving you lots of catching up to do. After all, nothing can jolt you back to reality quicker than an inbox bursting with 400+ e-mails that need answering!

Now imagine what it's like for your aging parents to go home after a vacation. If they don't have active social lives, they're returning not only to an empty nest but to empty days as well. The stark reality of being alone can hit them hard. I've seen Mom bear the full brunt of this whenever she and I complete a multi-week adventure to the other side of the planet: as soon as she gets home, she starts asking me, "When am I going to see you again?" Even though she knows that I visit her in Indianapolis every six to eight weeks, the post-vacation blues can make her feel anxious about our next get-together.

Reentry after a vacation can be difficult for anyone. (Sometimes I have a hard time coming home after just a long weekend trip!) Understand, though, that it can be especially tough on aging parents. So although you may be tempted to send your parents on their way back to their own home and return your focus to your life ASAP, take some time to make sure that your parents are managing their return to reality all right.

Reentry Tips Specific to Aging Parents

We each have our own bumpy spots on the path to getting back into our everyday routines after a vacation. Once you identify them and know exactly which things are going to be challenging (or drive you nuts!), dealing with them gets a *lot* easier.

Making sure Mom maintains her medication schedule is one of my biggest concerns with her, because if she gets off her pill regimen, there could be serious consequences. That's why I manage her pill schedule when we travel together (see chapter 4), because dealing with time changes and being off her usual routine can make it hard for her to keep track of what she needs to take when. And that's why I take steps to make sure that after a vacation she gets back into her usual routine for taking and managing prescriptions.

For example, I know that Mom *loathes* going to the drugstore to pick up refills. I also know that after a trip her enthusiasm for this task is decreased even more when she's exhausted from the travel itself (even sitting on an airplane is draining), possibly suffering from jet lag, and feeling lonely. So before we leave for vacation, I make sure she has enough pills to get her through the first week or so back at home after our trip. Then she doesn't have to run those errands right away—and she'll have plenty of medication to get her through the post-vacation blues.

Not every parent needs help with his or her medications, of course. But I think it's safe to say that *all* parents could benefit from some extra communication during the reentry period. Remember, you and your parent spent a few days (or weeks!) in each other's company. *You* may be ready to part ways and get back to being on your own, but your parent will always think of you as "my little girl" or "my little boy"—and when you're gone, he or she can feel your absence. So during that first week or so back, check in more often with your parent.

A few extra phone calls can have a huge effect. For example, when Mom and I aren't on a trip together or just back from one, I talk with her every morning. During the first few days after an extended vacation, though, I'll add on one or two calls at night, to make sure she's getting back out to see her friends and not sitting in her chair feeling all bummed out. These conversations don't have to last long: 5 or 10 minutes here and there are enough to remind your parent that he or she isn't alone (and that you're not going to disappear). And who can't spare an extra 10 or 20 minutes each week to talk with a parent?

When you chat with your parents on the phone, don't assume that they're getting back into their normal routines. You have to ask them specific questions about what they're doing. Find out when they're getting together with their friends, for example, or if they've resumed their usual activities. Returning to a normal routine through socializing, volunteering, going to church, or whatever else your parents like to do can help them snap out of any post-vacation sadness—just as getting busy with work often does for us adult children.

If you ever sense that your parent is suffering from depression or turning into a hermit, *talk about it*. Get your concerns out into the open! Remind your parent that the trip that just ended isn't the last vacation you'll ever take together, and maybe start chatting about future travel possibilities. Encouraging your parent to focus on the positive can help him or her avoid feeling blue.

At the same time, though, you don't want your parent to think that vacation was *so* "perfect" that real life seems awful in comparison! If your parent starts getting nostalgic about your vacation to the point that he or she can't enjoy everyday life, you may need to offer some balance. Even the best of vacations isn't awesome all of the time. When Mom starts down this path, I remind her of a moment on the trip where we were sniping at each other, using that example as a joke to remind her that vacations aren't always 100% pleasurable. Adding "How nice it must have been to get rid of me afterward!" always gets a laugh from Mom, who responds with, "No, no, that trip wasn't *that* bad! But okay, maybe it's not *so* awful to have some time on my own now." Another tactic I take is to tell her that I can see how not being around me all the time would make her depressed—a line that never fails to get a snort from her. The moment I hear her laughing, I know she's pulling out of the post-vacation blues—as am I. The truth is that I love being around Mom and miss her when we're not together. Even with nearly eight and a half million people, my current hometown of Manhattan can be a mighty lonely place, so I cherish my close connection with Mom.

If you suspect that your parent is feeling depressed, you need to deal with this issue and not try to let it resolve itself. But you'll have to figure out whether a direct approach or an indirect one works better with your parent. I know that if I ask my mom if she's depressed, she will always answer with an emphatic "No!" So instead I try to gather information that will give me a good sense of her frame of mind. I look for changes in her typical pre-vacation routine after we return, for example, and pay attention to how she's getting back to her favorite activities. In our morning chats I also ask her how she slept the previous night, because not sleeping can be a sign of depression. (It's also a symptom of jet lag, and I remind Mom that it takes time to recover from that.) In short, I try to ascertain how she's doing and gently encourage her to get back out there and see her friends.

Reentry Tips for Everyone

If I were allowed to give only a single piece of advice about coming home from vacation, it would be this: *give yourself a break.* Few people can roll straight from vacation back to their regular lives without a hitch, so anyone—regardless of age—who has trouble making that transition should not beat himself or herself up over it.

Think about everything that goes into a vacation: planning, packing, traveling, exploring, eating, drinking, sightseeing, walking—all sorts of activities that take place over days, weeks, and months. And they all end when your vacation ends. The shift from the anticipation and excitement stages of a vacation back to post-vacation regular life can be jarring for anyone.

As you make this adjustment, keep in mind that it's normal to feel a bit deflated after a vacation, particularly a fantastic one! We travel to learn about new cultures, see new sights, taste new foods, and have new experiences. *Of course* your normal routine might seem boring after all of that! So expect the boredom, but manage it by letting your mind occasionally linger on great memories from your trip—and remind yourself that doing your best in your everyday life, including your job, will enable you to go on more fun vacations in the future.

Once you've come to terms with the fact that a full return to regular life will take some time and effort, consider some of these suggestions for making that transition a bit easier.

Don't Overcommit Yourself

In chapter 8, I recommend not overscheduling yourself while on vacation. If you take the time to stop and smell the roses—or enjoy a glass of Chianti in an outdoor café, sit on a bench and watch passersby, or spend an afternoon lounging by the hotel pool—during your trip, both you and your parent will have a better time. Take the same approach post-travel, too: don't overcommit yourself once you return home. After all, being "too busy" is part of what we're trying to escape by going on vacation, right? (We've all relished doing "nothing" while on vacation as a break from the craziness of day-to-day life.) Rather than jump right back into your usual hectic life, take it easy for a while after you're home, so you can keep that relaxed feeling from vacation around a bit longer.

When planning a trip, try not to schedule anything too important during the first few days or week following vacation, particularly if you're coming back from overseas. Doing anything that requires a lot of energy or brain-power can be excruciating when you're supremely jet-lagged. (I've also found that my work isn't always up to my usual standards when I have jet lag.) So don't book that critical negotiation for your first day back from vacation. Instead, give yourself easy tasks—things that have been sitting on your plate for a while but haven't made it to the top of the priority list. Doing the easy stuff can make you feel good because you're still crossing action items off your list (but without too much trouble or worry).

Give yourself a break on the home front as well. For example, the days right after a vacation might be a great time to hand your dirty clothes over to a laundry service rather than wash them all yourself. Watch some goofy TV shows or cheesy movies while you pay your bills, file paperwork, and take care of other tasks that are easy to accomplish, won't hurt anything if not done to perfection, and don't require a significant amount of brainpower.

Adjust Your Day as Needed

Each person handles the post-vacation transition differently. Some lucky people are able to sleep well on planes, have no trouble syncing their internal clocks to local time, and laugh at the very idea of jet leg. Unfortunately, most of us (including me) do not fall into that category and often have rocky transitions back to our usual places and times. One key to managing that shift without going nuts is to be flexible.

When I return home from an overseas trip, I need about a week to re-adjust to the local time. This is particularly true when I've traveled to Asia, which is about half a day ahead of my usual time. During my first week back in New York City after a trip to China, for example, I wake up every morning at 3 or 4 a.m., which means that in the early afternoon I usually hit my wall and am barely functional (even if I'm still sitting at my desk). So during those first several post-vacation days, I schedule my important meetings and calls for the early morning, when I'm at my best. I don't try to do anything too strenuous or taxing when I'm struggling to keep my eyes open, let alone my brain engaged.

Take Short Naps

As the saying goes, "The best laid plans of mice and men often go awry"—and that holds true for many of our efforts to take it easy right after coming home from a vacation. Work beckons, family and friends need attention, and countless other unpredictable things come up that prevent us from having the flexible schedules we need to ease the transition to being back home. Under those circumstances, napping can be your best friend.

In chapter 8, I recommend taking a brief power nap shortly after reaching your destination, especially if you've been on a long-haul flight across several time zones. The same advice applies when returning to your hometown, too. Numerous scientific studies have proven what many people have known for a long time: a midafternoon power nap (lasting 30 or fewer minutes—more than that will have an adverse effect and lead to grogginess) can give someone a much-needed burst of energy. This technique can be useful if you're back from vacation and start to drag during the afternoon hours, especially if you have an important meeting or call in the afternoon that cannot be moved to the morning or to whenever you're at your best while you're trying to readjust. If you're able to take your power nap at home, great. If not, then improvise! When I'm working a consulting assignment at a client's location, for example, I'll schedule my lunch for later in the day (around 2 or 3 p.m.) and shut my door for a quick power nap (sometimes followed by an energizing walk around the outside of the building).

If you're lucky enough to have a totally flexible schedule, though, that doesn't mean you should nap whenever you like. Because she's retired, my mom has an open schedule that on the surface might seem ideal for readjusting after a big trip but can cause problems if not managed carefully.

Mom's flexibility makes it difficult for her to get back to her regular sleep pattern, because she can nod off for far too long during the day—which means she doesn't get to sleep until late at night. (After our last trip to China, for example, she needed *three weeks* to readjust to being in Indiana again!) So although it might seem that she'd have an easier time adjusting without a boss breathing down her neck to meet her work deadlines, the fact that she's not crazy busy makes it easier for her to close her eyes for "just a few minutes" that then turn into several hours.

Exercise

If you exercise regularly, you'll have no trouble getting back to your work-out routine. However, if you're like me and visit the gym only once a week (and that's in a good week!), you might have some trouble meeting this goal. If you push yourself to move your body, though, you'll readjust to home more easily and feel so much better in general. Forcing yourself to go to the gym can help with your energy levels and help you stay awake during "regular" hours when all you want to do is sleep. Combined with a power nap, exercise can give you the push you need to stay up later in the evening and get a better night's sleep—which in turn helps you recover from jet lag and get back to your regular schedule.

So follow Nike's advice and "Just do it!" You'll be amazed at the results. And who knows—perhaps you'll get into an exercise routine that lasts long after the jet lag has passed. (Unfortunately, that hasn't happened to me yet. But I can still dare to dream!)

Go Grocery Shopping

Sounds silly, doesn't it? But grocery shopping may be one of the best things you can do for yourself after a long trip. During your travels, you probably overindulged a bit. (After all, you were on vacation!) So when you return home, that's a great time to restock your pantry with healthy items to get back to your usual diet. Never shop when you're hungry, though, because hunger combined with a bit of jet lag could lead you straight to all the rich, crazy comfort foods that can keep you up at night. If you make yourself munch on a few celery stalks (instead of that mac-and-cheese you're craving!), you'll be able to get back to sleep faster.

That said, when you do go shopping, try to pick up a few things that remind you of your vacation. Don't go overboard, of course: if you've returned from Hawaii and are in the mood for papaya but it's not available at your usual store, for example, don't spend all day looking for it elsewhere. Sometimes it's fun to pick up a few foods that let you compare what you had on vacation with what you can get back home. I don't always try this myself, though: in China, Mom and I eat so much local food that all I crave when I get home is a big, fat, juicy American cheeseburger!

Organize and Share Your Photos

This is perhaps my favorite post-vacation activity! When you're feeling a little blue about the end of your vacation, take some time to wax nostalgic by organizing your trip photos and sharing them with friends via e-mail and your favorite social media sites (e.g., Facebook, Instagram, Twitter). I make sure to limit myself to no more than an hour a day of this—otherwise I'd spend all my time on Facebook posting and chatting with friends about my adventures and all the fun I had!

Physical scrapbooks are another great way to preserve and share trip memories, especially with aging parents who might not be tech savvy (or, in the case of my mom, don't have Internet access at home). In addition to photos of the various sights you and your parent saw (and of the foods you ate), you can include notes about where you went, what you did, and how you felt during your trip. I make scrapbooks after every trip with Mom: not only do they bring her a lot of joy, but they also reinforce my memories of what we did on vacation. Have you ever drawn a blank when someone asks you what you did on your recent vacation? I typically find that I do so many fun things on trips with Mom that it's hard to keep them all straight! So chronicling the adventures helps me remember them better.

Because putting a scrapbook together can take some time (I snap *hundreds* of pictures when we're on vacation, so I usually need a few weeks to make a book afterward), consider sending your parent copies of a dozen or so shots shortly after you get home. The prints I send to Mom and the journals we keep during our trip (see chapter 8) let her share the fun travel tales with her friends right away (as I do with mine on Facebook) while waiting for me to finish the scrapbook.

Write!

My daily schedule includes a lot of writing: I write posts for my blog on management topics, I write content for my travel-oriented blog, I always have at least one book in process, and I write articles for several trade magazines. In short, I write *a lot*. With all of this professional writing on my plate, I find it tough to make the time to keep a personal journal, even though journaling is incredibly cathartic and helpful when my mind is rushing around and I'm stressed because I have so much going on. One thing I love about being on vacation is having the time (and inspiration!) to keep a regular journal during my trip, and I highly recommend doing so while on your own travels.

During your vacation, write about what you did, where you went, who you met, how you felt—put all those feelings and impressions down in a journal. If your parent is up for it, bring a journal for him or her to write in, too. Writing hurts my mom's hand, though, so I often give her copies of my journal (but not the pages on which I complain about her or use language she doesn't approve of!). When you want to dispel some of those post-vacation blues, your journal can take you back to the great vacation you shared with your parent.

And there's no reason to stop journaling once you're back home. You may find it a great way to organize the thoughts swirling around in your head. If you're feeling particularly adventurous, consider starting a blog about your travels, your everyday life, or whatever you like! Blogging is easier than you think (if you need help getting started, look online for tutorials or check out local continuing-education courses), and once you get into it, you'll be amazed at how rewarding it can be to commit your thoughts to writing.

Make Plans with Friends

When returning from vacation, it's easy to turn the bulk of your attention to catching up at the office and taking care of your home and family (especially if you have children). But focusing only on those things can quickly make you feel overburdened and exhausted. Don't allow that to happen! Instead, make it a point to schedule some good quality time with friends, even if it's for a quick coffee or lunch together. Your social life is a vital part of your daily routine, too. Sharing your vacation stories with good friends who "ooh!" and "ahh!" in the same places you did is tremendous fun and will make you happier about being home again from even the best of vacations!

Pamper Yourself

When easing back into your daily routine, why not do something kind for yourself? Schedule a massage, manicure, or pedicure, for example. Or read fluff magazines (a supreme indulgence for me!), start a new book, or simply go to a park and people-watch. Do whatever offers you inner peace and reflection—and makes you thankful to be in the here and now. This is important during any given week, but it's even more so when reentering your regular life after a great vacation.

Pampering yourself can be as simple as giving yourself an extra day of rest before heading back to work. So many people who come home late on Sunday night are at the office the next morning at 9 a.m.—and totally tired and unable to do their best work. (I get exhausted *thinking* about that quick turnaround!) If you want a full week of vacation, for example, try for a Saturday-to-Saturday time frame so you have Sunday to relax and adjust before going back to the office on Monday. The easier you make the return for yourself, the better you'll be able to get back into the swing of things with minimal hassle.

Plan Your Next Trip

Hatching a plan for your next vacation will give you and your parent something to look forward to—a great way to get over the post-vacation blues! Nothing gets my heart racing like planning a trip, and knowing that another adventure is on the horizon helps both Mom and me adjust to our regular lives. (Personally, I *always* need something travel-related to look forward to—even if it's just a long weekend away.) In fact, Mom and I love travel planning so much that we usually start brainstorming about our next trip *during the return flight for our just-completed trip!* We discuss what we liked about the vacation we just took, because understanding what made that trip so great can help us choose where to go next. We don't necessarily come up with our next destination during this first conversation, but we at least begin to identify some of the elements we want in our next trip together.

Be a Tourist at Home

It's pretty easy to take our own backyards for granted. We'll travel halfway across the country or the world to see beautiful churches, take in gorgeous scenery, and eat exotic food. But we often forget to search for excitement in the next town over or even around the corner from home. Don't underestimate the local possibilities for adventure!

Most museums have rotating exhibits, for example, so buy a membership to a nearby institution and visit it every few months. Try that new restaurant that just opened, too. And check out the arts and entertainment section of your local paper and commit to going to one new event (no matter how obscure it is) each month. Even if you end up not enjoying a particular exhibit, meal, show, or whatever, you'll still have fun getting out of your routine every now and then.

I grew up in southern Indiana and felt there was "nothing to do" there, even after I moved from a small town to Indianapolis, the capital. Since moving away at the age of 29, though, I have a different perspective. Now when I return to Indiana, I finally see all the cool sites that were there all along, and Mom and I explore them together. It's easy to fall into a routine and miss the opportunities right next to us. (Heck, I have to be careful not to let that happen even in the amazingly exciting city of New York, where I live now!) Don't let that sense of travel adventure fade because you've returned home. Get out there and keep exploring!

Final Thoughts

We can learn many lessons from our travels by asking ourselves one simple question: "What great things about my vacation do I want to incorporate into my everyday life?" Maybe you find that you want to take more chances. Or maybe you've discovered an interest in the exploration of new cuisines, cultures, or landscapes. As a chronic overscheduler, I always come home from vacation vowing to relax and not to overbook myself. Unfortunately, I haven't yet succeeded in making this change permanent in my life. But I *have* managed to slow down for at least a couple of weeks after my trip, and I've truly enjoyed lingering a bit longer in the peacefulness of my most recent vacation. So take some time to identify the best qualities of your vacation—then make a conscious effort to incorporate them into your life at home.

Remember, you and your parent both need time to readjust to being back home after a vacation. You have to deal with time differences, schedule shifts, and getting back into the daily routines that made you need a vacation in the first place! The last thing you want to do when you return to reality is make yourself feel bad about whatever it is you think you should be accomplishing. So keep in mind that everything—even adjusting to your own familiar schedules—takes time. If you and your parent can be patient with yourselves (and with each other), you'll soon be back to normal and planning your next trip together!

TRAVELING WITH BOTH CHILDREN AND AGING PARENTS

And that's the wonderful thing about family travel:
it provides you with experiences that will remain
locked forever in the scar tissue of your mind.
—Dave Barry

Mom and I often joke about being "trapped" with each other while on vacation together, but the truth is that these shared experiences have far-reaching positive impacts on our lives, and we wouldn't trade them for anything. Throughout this book I've dissected many of the "hows" and the "how nots" of adult children traveling with their aging parents. But that's not the only possible scenario for intergenerational travel. In fact, many of those adult children belong to the "sandwich generation" who are responsible for the care of both their parents and their children who are still at home. A recent AARP report found that 44% of 45- to 55-year-olds had at least one living parent and one child under the age of 21—a number that is only expected to grow.

In a 2011 study on multigenerational travel, Preferred Hotel Group found that 40% of the participants (which correlates to 20.8 million individuals or households in the U.S.) had, in the year prior to the survey, gone on a trip that included three or more generations, and 40% of those travelers had vacationed outside the U.S. Most of the survey respondents planned vacations around major life events such as anniversaries, birthdays, and weddings, and many of these regard multigenerational travel as a way to connect with other family members, especially those who live far from each other.

More than preceding generations, baby boomers have the money to take trips with their children—and their grandchildren. They're searching for togetherness and meaningful experiences, and planning a vacation that meets these criteria and appeals to the interests of multiple generations poses unique challenges. I understand this well: with an eight-decade age difference between my mother and her grandchildren, our family vacations require significant planning (and some compromise, too!) to ensure that everyone has a good time.

First Thoughts

Before you can select a vacation destination and activities, you must first understand what your fellow vacationers can do—both mentally and physically. In chapter 2, I discuss these considerations in detail where they concern traveling with an aging parent. But when you're planning a trip that includes both young *and* old, you'll need to consider the abilities and limitations of multiple generations.

If your parents are in excellent health, then your young children's abilities might set the pace for your activities. As your parents age, though, their physical limitations may increase while your children become more active. When planning a trip, don't forget to factor in rest periods for *everyone*, regardless of age—even if your children are older, for example, and no longer need naps. If you're extremely lucky, your children and your parents will be able to handle the same activity level. Odds are, though, that your vacation will be a fine balancing act among the needs and interests of different age groups.

Part of the challenge of understanding our parents' physical capabilities lies in how easy it is for us not to recognize when they may be slowing down or to fail to realize that they are vulnerable. This point was driven home for me about 15 years ago when my parents and I vacationed in Montauk, on the eastern tip of Long Island. My dad had ridden horses all his life, but during this particular trip being on horseback for an extended period of time hurt his knees and back. I was shocked to see my father in such pain from something he had done many times before. How could my "John Wayne" be unable to ride a horse? When did he become fragile? This ride was a stunning wake-up call and, sadly, Dad's last ride, because being on a horse had become too uncomfortable for him.

Interestingly, when our parents have trouble keeping up with us, we can find that more irritating than when our children need a break. Perhaps that's because we expect these challenges from a child but not from our parents. Or maybe we're reluctant to acknowledge a parent's limitations because they indicate that we, too, are getting older—and who wants to admit *that*? As I learned during that trip to Montauk, it's easy to forget that our parents' abilities change with age; we tend to assume that they can still do all that they used to be able to do when we were younger.

So as you start to plan a multigenerational vacation, think carefully about the expectations you have for your parents and for your children (and for yourself, too!). By factoring in each participant's physical abilities, especially their stamina, you'll have a better chance of keeping your expectations in line with reality and thus avoid disappointment if you don't manage to cram in all the activities on your list. Taking *all* of those variables into consideration during your trip planning will help ensure a better vacation experience—for everyone involved.

What to Look for in a Destination

Before exploring potential destinations, ask all participants what they want to do on this vacation together. If someone says, "I don't care," don't accept that answer. Trust me: *everyone* cares. So keep pushing your family members for their input. This information will help you plan a vacation that strikes a good balance between activity and relaxation—and the input will take some of the pressure off you (because you won't be solely responsible for everyone's happiness). Also talk to *everyone* who's going on the trip, regardless of his or her age. Even young kids have their own ideas, and including them in the planning process can build their excitement about the upcoming trip.

Once you have a better understanding of what your family members want to do while on vacation, search for destinations that have a variety of activities (with different physical demands) as well as interesting options for relaxation. At these sorts of places, the more active set can run as hard as they want while the members of your group who want or need a more relaxing vacation will also have a good time. Having multiple options also makes it possible for people to vary their activity levels day by day. So, for example, someone who originally planned to relax by the pool but decides to join the others for a day of more strenuous activity can do so.

When evaluating destinations, make a list of priorities to help you narrow down your options. For example, here are some of the features Mom and I value having at or near our accommodations when we travel:

- Places that are good for relaxing and chilling out (e.g., beach, pool, seating areas)

- Physical activities that suit our abilities (for example, walking paths rather than hardcore hiking trails)

- Activities that the whole family can enjoy together (regardless of age)

- Art galleries, museums, and other wheelchair-accessible sites

- Spas

- Quick access to the hotel (for when someone needs to take a break)

That last item is important for both young children and aging parents. (And for me, too! There are definitely times when I need a quick power nap.) The preparations for traveling with multiple generations entail accommodating everyone's capabilities—and that includes making it possible for anyone in your group (regardless of age) to take breaks as needed.

Because they usually have a wide variety of activities organized by age and activity levels, all-inclusive resorts and cruise ships are worth a close look. Planning a vacation at one of these places can reduce the amount of planning you need to do: because the activities are all in one place, you don't have to do a lot of "what to do in the local area" research. Features and amenities can vary wildly, so be sure to compare several places before booking a stay anywhere. Some of the features you might find include bar areas where adults can congregate once the kiddies have gone to bed, a wide range of food options to appeal to picky eaters of any age, and adults-only pools (in addition to all-ages pools). Also, all-inclusive places are sometimes less expensive than other vacation options, because they don't have à la carte fees for individual activities. (Your wallet will be happy about this feature if, like my brother's twins, your children fixate on a particular activity and want to repeat it over and over!)

At whatever destination Mom and I choose, I always look for hotels with on-site relaxation spots (such as a beach or a pool) or lounging areas with beautiful views. (I typically don't count spas as "relaxation spots," because their high price tags exclude them from the "daily activity to unwind" category—and make me feel stressed about paying the bill when I return home!) Even when we have our noses buried in our books, Mom and I still love to surround ourselves with new sights and sounds. An outdoor setting—especially one where we can watch the sunset, with a cocktail in hand, of course!—is always a top priority on our amenities list, and I usually upgrade our hotel room to get a balcony or view of water, mountains, or other scenery.

As long as I chose a location wisely, everyone is usually happy, regardless of age. The activities that are available influence each person's "happiness" factor, though, so be sure that your trip planning includes assessing the available options. Ensuring that your destination has a wide range of possibilities that include physical activities for those who prefer to be out and about all day long, as well as laid-back options for those who prefer to take it easy and relax, will go a long way toward keeping everyone happy.

Flying with Children

With the right planning, traveling by plane with an aging parent can be accomplished without too much stress. Adding children to the mix requires somewhat different preparations. But those, too, aren't as difficult as you might think (or fear!).

Ticket Options for Children

If you're flying and your child is under two years old, current guidelines permit you to hold him or her in your lap for the duration of the flight rather than purchase a separate seat for the child. Your child will need a special "lap child ticket" (which may carry some fees but is still considerably less expensive than a regular ticket) that should be purchased at the time you arrange any adult tickets, and at the airport you'll have to provide proof of your child's age. Note that airlines have varying rules about these types of tickets (for example, most limit them to one per parent-child pair—so a parent traveling with two children under the age of two must purchase a regular ticket for at least one of them), so check your particular airline's requirements carefully.

Once children reach two years of age, they need their own seats, and they must be in them during takeoff and landing. Airlines typically require children under the age of five to be accompanied by a parent or guardian. The cutoff for unaccompanied travel varies from airline to airline, though. As always, check your airline's rules.

Checked Luggage

Most airlines do not charge for wheelchairs, strollers, or car seats that are checked as luggage. (In light of increasing baggage fees, though, don't count on that to last forever.) I recommend gate-checking these items when possible, though, so that they are readily available when you land and need to make the long hike to the baggage claim area—and so they can avoid rough treatment from baggage handlers.

Moving through the Airport

I've mentioned elsewhere (see chapter 7) that moving through airports with an aging parent can be challenging, particularly if your parent has difficulty walking. Traveling with small children at the same time increases the challenges. Using an airline-provided wheelchair (reserved in advance) can help your parent move around more easily without getting exhausted. A wheelchair can also usually tote your carry-on bags, too—thus freeing both your hands and your attention for child-wrangling. Another great perk? Wheelchair users typically take an expedited lane through security and passport control, which makes the whole security-screening process much smoother and quicker (and *almost* makes it a pleasant experience).

Security Screenings

The TSA has specific requirements for bringing liquids, gels, and aerosols in carry-on bags: those items must be in containers that hold no more than 3.4 ounces each, and all of those containers must fit into one quart-size zip-top bag. (See chapters 3 and 5 for more details on the regulations.) However, medically required liquids for children (including baby formula, breast milk, food, and medications) *are* allowed in carry-on bags in amounts exceeding 3.4 ounces in reasonable quantities for the flight, and they do not need to fit in a quart-size zip-top bag. If you're traveling with such items, inform the TSA officer at the entrance to the screening area and don't send them through the X-ray machine undeclared.

Just as TSA regulations permit seniors 75 and older to keep their shoes on while going through security, they also permit children 12 and younger to do the same. Not unexpectedly, all children's toys and child-related items (such as diaper bags, strollers, baby carriers, car seats, and baby slings) must go through the X-ray machine. A child who sets off an alarm in the walk-through metal detector may be asked to walk through it additional times; a child who continues to set off alarms will probably be swabbed (usually on his or her hands) rather than subjected to a regular pat-down. Any child who repeatedly sets off metal detectors or seems suspicious in any way, however, may be required to walk through a full-body scanner.

If your child uses a wheelchair for medical reasons, inform the TSA officers if your child can either be carried by a parent or guardian or walk alone through the metal detector. If neither option is possible, a TSA agent will do a pat-down search of your child in his or her wheelchair.

Travel Paperwork

Children under 18 usually do not need to show ID when checking in and going through security. Travelers of all ages, however, must have a valid passport when leaving the United States. For children who are 15 or younger at the time they receive (or renew) a passport, passports are good for five years. Because children can change so much in appearance during this short period, their passports may receive a bit of extra scrutiny from officials. (For example, my three-year-old nieces now look very different from their passport pictures, which were taken when they were infants, and it's quite funny to watch passport control agents look at them carefully. I've suggested to my brother that he get new passports for the girls, but he insists on using the current ones until they expire!)

Meanwhile, to thwart child abductions, the U.S. Customs and Border Protection (CBP) agency strongly suggests that an adult traveling with a child who is not accompanied by both parents carry a notarized letter authorizing this travel. The note should be written by the nontraveling parent or, if the child is traveling with other relatives or friends, by both parents. The CBP website includes this statement as a template for such notes: "I acknowledge that my wife/husband/etc. is traveling out of the country with my son/daughter/group. He/She/They has/have my permission to do so."

Unaccompanied Minors

If your child is flying alone, when you book the ticket you must specify which adult (a parent, guardian, or other designated adult) will escort him or her to the departure gate and which adult will pick up the child at the arrival gate on the other end. At the point of departure, the designated adult must take the child to the departure gate and remain there until the flight has left the ground. If the child has a connecting flight, an airline representative will assist him or her en route. At the arrival point, the designated adult should report to the airport one hour before the flight's scheduled arrival in order to obtain a gate pass. The adult must present valid identification before the minor will be released into his or her custody.

In-Flight Entertainment

As when traveling with your parent, be sure to bring along plenty of entertainment options when traveling with a child. Pack books, games, small toys—whatever will keep your little one occupied and content while you're in transit, particularly if it's a long trip. If you have one, I highly recommend bringing along an iPad or other tablet, because it's a great entertainment option for both adults and children. My mom loves to play solitaire and hearts on her iPad, and my nieces use iOS apps for drawing and coloring. Don't forget to load a boatload of movies on your tablet, too!

Childcare, Finances, and Budgeting

Talking about money is always tough, but it's something you and your parents should do well before hitting the road together. You'll need to cover the usual territory, such as whether the costs for shared accommodations will be split down the middle between you and your parents, and who will pay for meals and activities. When children are along for the trip, too, you and your parents need to discuss babysitting as well.

Will you expect your parents to babysit while you're exploring on your own? If so, will you be compensating your parents for this work (with cash, perhaps, or by covering some of the trip costs)? Keep in mind that babysitting is a *job*—and your parents may prefer to spend most of the trip relaxing, something that's hard to do while looking after young children. So don't assume that your parents will be happy to babysit for you while on vacation. Talk to them about this possibility and what payment you can offer them (beyond the joy and fun of spending quality time with their grandchildren, of course!) for looking after your kids.

Once everyone agrees on who's contributing what to the vacation expenses, you can start looking for the best deals on airfare, lodging, trip activities, and other elements of your trip. I recommend doing this research both on aggregator websites (such as Expedia and Travelocity) and on the service providers' own sites. Here are a few more ways to look for travel deals:

- Do an Internet search for the provider's name and the word "discount" to see if any coupons are available online—you never know what you may find.

- Ask your parents if they belong to any organizations that provide discounts, such as AARP, AAA, or travel clubs such as Costco.

- Before making major purchases, check with the vendor for senior discounts. They are becoming increasingly rare, though some companies still offer them.

- Consider consulting travel agents, too, because they can sometimes find perks to add to your trip and prices that are lower than what you can find on your own.

- Check for hotel, dining, and entertainment deals and coupons on websites such as Groupon, Entertainment, and Amazon Local.

- Look for hotels that offer complimentary breakfasts or have in-room kitchens so you have the option of eating one meal each day in your room. Not having to dine out for every meal can dramatically cut your food expenses.

- If any travelers in your group need to use the Internet or send e-mail during your trip, search for accommodations that offer free or low-cost Wi-Fi. Hotel connections tend to be more secure than those in Internet cafes and at public Wi-Fi hot spots.

If you're renting a car, your group will have to decide how to share the associated costs and responsibilities. For starters, you'll need some sort of insurance. Coverage offered by the rental company can be *very* expensive (particularly if you're on an extended vacation), so before you start your vacation, find out if you already have coverage through your regular car insurance company back home. (Because I live in New York City and don't own a car, Mom and I put her name down as the primary driver when we rent a car together, so we have coverage through her carrier at home.) Credit card companies often provide insurance for rentals paid for with their cards, so check on this option, too. (See chapter 10 for detailed advice on car rental insurance.)

When we rent cars together, Mom and I have an understanding that the person who gets a ticket is the one who has to pay for it. (Mom is quite the speed demon, so this arrangement serves as an incentive for her to slow down.) If we're in an accident, though, we've agreed to split the costs. Fortunately, our on-vacation driving records are clean (so far!).

We also agree to split most meals and activities. If I order something outrageously pricey, though, then Mom pays only her portion of the cost. For example, I love seeing live shows, but she is not a fan of the crazy prices most Broadway theaters charge. So when we go to a show, she usually buys dinner beforehand and I pick up the tickets. Similarly, if I want to go to an expensive restaurant, I'll foot the bill.

There is little that Mom and I *haven't* discussed when it comes to our travel finances. This open approach allows us to establish our expectations before we leave home. Then when we're on vacation, we can both relax and enjoy ourselves—without anyone getting mad when the check arrives!

Planning a Vacation Everyone Can Enjoy

Getting everyone to agree on activities can be tough with a big group. (Even Mom and I don't always agree about what we want to do when it's just the two of us!) So don't try to plan out every moment of every day together. Remember, you selected a destination with a lot of things to do so that everyone can have a great time on this trip. Also keep in mind that people have different schedules and different preferences (for example, I love to get up early and scout out cafes, whereas Mom prefers to sleep in and have a late, leisurely breakfast). So encourage everyone in your group to be flexible.

Just as you discussed trip finances with all the vacation participants, have a discussion with everyone about the activities you would like to do as a group, and be sure to space those activities out during your trip so they don't exhaust anyone. If you'd like everyone to share a particular meal each day, remember that booking all of those meals together can be challenging if everyone's on different schedules (for example, if you have both night owls and early risers in your group). Instead, consider planning a few meals with everyone—such as one or two nights where the whole family cooks or checks out a local restaurant together. Getting everyone to agree on a particular cuisine can be tough, so if you're dining out, your best bet may be to find a restaurant with enough variety to accommodate everyone's tastes. Pick a middle-of-the-road restaurant for when everyone's eating together, and save the places with fancy, crazy cuisines for outings that include only the more adventurous diners.

When Mom and I travel with my brother and his family, usually we all eat dinner together every night and do activities throughout the day in smaller groups. When we all want to do something together, we book private tours with our own van and driver. (A group discount for four adults can make the prices for those fairly reasonable.) Personalized arrangements make sense for our group, because we typically need extra time to explore the sites with a wheelchair and two strollers, to make frequent bathroom stops (it's impossible to get two children and four adults on the same bathroom schedule!), and to have lunch or a snack while we're out (my mom and my nieces are all slow eaters). Booking private tours also allows us to adjust our schedule on the fly if anyone needs or wants to return to the hotel immediately. And a private van has enough room for all the stuff we bring on day trips, including a wheelchair, two strollers, snacks, water, and entertainment options for the children if they get bored.

During our multigenerational trips, my family builds in a lot of rest time between activities so we can each catch our breath. (After all, adults of *all* ages need a break after a few hours of pushing wheelchairs and strollers!) I think this "relaxed scheduling" is the secret to our successful vacations, because it helps everyone in our group avoid exhaustion. Exhaustion is never 100% avoidable, of course, but planning for breaks (and naps!) helps us stave off the crabbiness that typically accompanies it. And because we pick destinations and accommodations with lots of things to do, those in our group who want to keep running can do so while the others rest and recharge.

Activities the Whole Family Can Do Together

When was the last time your entire family played a board game together? Being on vacation is a great excuse to break out Candy Land, Pictionary, or another old favorite. Bring along a board game (or two) for some great entertainment one evening; puzzles that the whole family can work on together are another fun option. (Be sure to bring some games and puzzles that are accessible to all age ranges in your group.) You'll get to spend quality time together, and if bad weather makes outings unpleasant, you'll be glad for something else to do. Because games and puzzles are sometimes bulky, consider bringing items that you won't mind leaving behind. You can always fill that empty space in your suitcase with purchases you make during your trip!

My brother and I love to cook, and his daughters love to "help" us. So if it's possible, we'll all cook one meal together during our trip. (Well, Mom sits with a glass of Bailey's and watches the rest of us do all the work, but she still participates in the fun!) Cooking can be especially relaxing after a hard day of sightseeing, so if anyone in your group enjoys cooking, try to arrange your lodging and schedule to accommodate a stay-at-home meal one evening.

Don't Forget Your Sense of Adventure

If you're convinced that bringing your extended family together for a vacation will be an awful experience, I'm sure that will be the case for you. On the other hand, if you make up your mind in advance to have a great time, your multigenerational vacation will fulfill your expectations. Much of our "reality" is based on what we decide to feel and believe, and this is especially true when it comes to travel. I won't kid you—travel *can* be difficult at times. But a healthy sense of humor and ample good spirits will make it better. So before you turn on your computer and start exploring potential destinations, first make sure you break out your sense of adventure!

Traveling with your extended family can be one of the most pleasant ways for all involved to reconnect on a deeper level with each other. It's wondrous to see the world through the eyes of children as well as from the perspective of adults of various ages. If you bring a positive attitude and an open mind, you'll be better prepared to deal with any challenges that do pop up during a multigenerational vacation.

SENIOR-TO-SENIOR ADVICE ON TRAVELING WITH ADULT CHILDREN

I have found out that there ain't no surer way to find out whether you like people or hate them than to travel with them.
—Mark Twain

Throughout this book, I've discussed travel from the perspective of the adult child helping an aging parent prepare for and go on a vacation and settle back in at home afterward. There are two sides to every coin, however, and it's important to consider the aging parent's point of view, too.

Depending on your relationship with your parent, you may find yourself assuming the dominant role and doing more "telling" rather than "involving" in the trip-planning process. In addition, if you already manage aspects of your parent's day-to-day life (such as medicines, finances, etc.) or if you have children, assuming an authoritarian approach to your vacations together might be an easy next step for you. Be careful, though, not to dictate the plans so much that your parents become reluctant to travel with you. Always keep their perspective in mind. After all, if you're irritated when your parents still treat you like a child (see chapter 6 for more about this sort of lingering emotional baggage), your parents are probably bothered when you do the same to them.

Experience is a great teacher, and it's taught me a great deal through the thousands of miles that Mom and I have traveled together. I've learned, for example, that my constantly telling her what to do can cause her severe anxiety—which then results in a horrible trip for both of us. So instead we've settled into a nice routine in which I do most of the planning and periodically give her updates and discuss options with her. Because she has faith that I'll keep her in the loop, she isn't afraid to speak up and voice her opinion on what she wants to do or not do.

Intergenerational travel is most successful when such conflicts are avoided from the start. Including your parent's preferences, expectations, and concerns in the trip planning will help you both have an awesome time together—so much so that you may start planning your next trip while on your way home from the first! Throughout this book I've detailed how you can prepare to travel with your aging parents. In this chapter, however, I discuss what your parents can expect when traveling with you.

To gather this information, I surveyed senior readers (age 55 and up) of the *Travel with Aging Parents* blog (and Mom, too, of course!) about their travels with their adult children. Their stories described fond memories, cringeworthy moments, and plenty of laughs. (Reading through them, I remembered how much I love to travel with my mom and found myself wanting to hop on a plane with her right then and there!) Some of their comments have been lightly edited for clarity here, but for the most part these words come straight from the horses' mouths (so to speak!).

If you're an adult child thinking about traveling with your parents, this chapter will give you some insight on the older generation's thoughts about such a trip. Most of this book is targeted to you (though of course there's nothing wrong with sharing it with your parents), but this part is specifically addressed to your parents. So I encourage you to show them this chapter and ask them to read it, regardless of whether they read the rest of the book.

If you're a parent considering taking a trip with your adult child, this chapter will help you see some of the many positive aspects of travel in general. You'll also get a sense of what to expect when you travel with your child—the high points as well as the challenges—and great advice for overcoming common problems that can pop up when you're on the road. Remember, these questions were answered by seniors who've traveled with their adult children and lived to tell the tales of their adventures. If they can do it, *so can you!*

"What do you like most about traveling in general?"

I wasn't surprised to find "seeing new sights" and "experiencing different cultures and new adventures" topping the list of what survey respondents like most about traveling. (After all, if we wanted the same old, same old, we could stay at home, right?) Here are a few additional things respondents love about travel:

- "I see something new every time I travel the same route." *(Manuel, 59, Texas)*
- "Casinos! Shopping!" *(Dora, 82, Texas)*
- "Hotels with indoor pools!" *(Sally, 72, Indiana)*
- "To enjoy a break from work and have fun." *(Deborah, 64, Georgia)*
- "Not having to make my bed every day." *(Chris, 66, Oregon)*
- "The peace that comes with time off from work." *(Sylvia, 57, Rhode Island)*
- "No cooking." *(Sharon, 58, Texas)*
- "Eating new foods (and drinking my first Guinness at the Storehouse in Dublin)!" *(Stacy, 58, Washington)*

These are all great responses, but the one from Diane (70) in New Jersey best describes my own favorite part about traveling in general:

- "Everything!"

The key to having a fantastic vacation is to keep reminding yourself of all these great reasons to travel (they are particularly important when you encounter problems getting to your destination). Whether you travel by plane, car, or other mode of transportation, assume that problems will arise en route—and figure out ahead of time what you'll do if that happens. When you're armed with a plan *before* you walk out the door, an unplanned hotel stay along the way to your destination becomes another part of your adventure. After all, seeing new sights is near the top of everyone's list of top reasons to travel, and with the right frame of mind an unexpected stop in an airport or city en route can be considered an extra bit of sightseeing!

"What do you like most about traveling with your adult child?"

In their answers to this question, many respondents highlighted the bonding and memory-building experiences that they shared with their adult children while on the road. Mom wrote, "Traveling with an adult child can give you some of the best memories of your life and possibly some of the best you'll ever have with your child. I love seeing the capable woman my daughter has grown into."

Another recurring theme was that most (though not all) of the adult children handled the travel details, much to their parents' delight. Stacy (58) from Washington explained, "[My daughter] made all the travel arrangements. I was amazed at her ability to schedule and coordinate." And Mom had this to say on the subject: "It's just too overwhelming nowadays to figure out all the options. I just want to go have fun—not deal with the planning. My daughter enjoys it, so I let *her* deal with all of that!"

Here are a few of the other answers I received to this question:

- "[My daughter and her husband] enjoy seeing sights and showing their children places we visited when they were little." *(CB, 66, Oregon)*

- "Learning to be friends with my son." *(Janet, 69, Texas)*

- "Bonding time as adults. It's wonderful." *(Sandy, 74, Texas)*

- "[My daughter] shows me things I wouldn't otherwise see." *(Barbara, 83, Massachusetts)*

- "Sharing driving. Spending time with each other away from home." *(Sally, 72, Indiana)*

- "Being together. I don't like living away from my children." *(Frances, 83, Louisiana)*

- "The bond that comes from spending time [with my son] is priceless." *(Sylvia, 57, Rhode Island)*

- "The memories and conversations we share." *(Manuel, 59, Texas)*

We all travel in order to have new experiences. But who you share those experiences with is as important as your destination. Mom and I have traveled together so much that we don't have to entertain each other or talk constantly. We're both fine being quiet together sometimes (say, at an outdoor café) and soaking in the local culture and sights in silence. These shared experiences give us more to talk about during our trip and enrich our conversations (and our appreciation of our "everyday" lives) even more when we're back home.

"What has surprised you most about traveling with your adult child?"

Here's one important reason why aging parents and their adult children should travel together: no matter how well you think you know each other, there's a strong possibility that you'll learn something new while exploring new places together. For example, are your children doing what they want to do with their lives? What would they do if money were no object? What big goals are still on their plates? During our trip to Australia in early 2013, Mom and I had a big "goals" conversation that resulted in the creation of the *Travel with Aging Parents* blog, the precursor to this book. Mom's insight—and her encouragement to "just go for it!"—were instrumental in my decision to pursue this project.

In her response to this question, Mom said she was most surprised by my patience: "Valerie's not known for her patience, but for the most part she's wonderful with me while we're on vacation. It makes it fun to be around her when she relaxes."

Several other respondents expressed surprise at their children's "ability to adapt" and "flexibility." I also found it heartwarming to read about parents who realized through travel how much they and their children have in common and who learned surprising things about each other. I experienced the wonder of such discoveries during my first trip with Mom. Previously, I had never thought of her as having any hopes or dreams beyond being my mother, and it was only through our conversations while on the road that I learned she had wanted to be a pharmacist before my oldest brother came along!

As an adult child reading through the survey responses, I found it fascinating to learn what members of my parents' generation think of their children. Here are some of the other things that surprised respondents during trips with their adult children:

- "Talking about personal issues—things I thought she would talk with her mother about." *(Manuel, 59, Texas)*

- "That they are adults, not the kids I see them as." *(Oralia, 61, Texas)*

- "How much I enjoy watching them have fun. It is like watching them as big kids." *(Patricia, 67, Georgia)*

- "[My daughter's] willingness to try new foods." *(Stacy, 58, Washington)*

- "How much we are alike." *(Barbara, 83, Massachusetts)*

- "The sheer joy of [my son's] laugh and being there to hear it in person." *(Janet, 69, Texas)*

- "How open and honest we were." *(Sandy, 74, Texas)*

- "It surprises me that we get along so well cramped together in the car." *(Sandra, 64, Alabama)*

- "[My daughter's] boundless energy." *(Myrna, 73, Florida)*

If you're still on the fence about taking a trip with your adult child, I hope that these comments will compel you to try it at least once. Maybe you'll be like Sally (72) of Indiana, who took a chance on a trip with her second daughter and made a pleasant discovery: "The one child I butted heads with the most while raising her is now my second favorite traveling companion (after her dad)!" If Sally had held on to the past, she might have missed discovering what a wonderful person her daughter had become!

"What do you like least about traveling with your adult child?"

Airport hassles and flight delays were mentioned in many responses to this question. They plague travel in general (whether or not adult children are involved), though, and annoy pretty much everyone (check out chapter 7 for advice on getting there and back again with your sanity intact!). Interestingly, several survey respondents indicated that they loved "everything" about traveling with their adult children—except, as Nancy (55) from Florida, pointed out, "the laundry when I get home"!

At the same time, quite a few respondents found their adult children to be bossy with them at times. (Attention, children: let's try to keep that in check on future trips with our parents!) Here are some of the other challenges highlighted by the survey:

- "[My daughter] knows me too well. I can't get away with anything." *(Barbara, 83, Massachusetts)*
- "Sometimes they forget that I get tired more easily." *(Reta, 60, Alabama)*
- "I don't like it when it's time to go home. I miss everyone and wish we could be together always." *(Frances, 83, Louisiana)*
- "My son and I are a great travel duo. It's the input of *other* adult travel members that causes friction." *(Alicia, 62, Florida)*
- "[My daughter] sometimes walked too fast and got ahead of me. I eventually caught up, but by then she had caught her breath and was ready to continue on again." *(Stacy, 58, Washington)*
- "[My children's] schedules can run a little past my bedtime!" *(Debbie, 55, Michigan)*

Edna (64) from North Carolina complained that her daughter always expected her to pay for everything and also assumed that she would babysit the grandkids. Before taking another trip with her daughter, Edna may want to have her children read chapter 12, which tackles discussing finances (and babysitting) to iron out major differences in expectations *before* hitting the road together. One respondent emphasized this point in her survey answers: "Have the $$ conversation before you go," recommends Debbie (55) from Michigan.

My favorite comment about the least-liked aspect about traveling with adult children was this gem from CB (66) of Oregon: "Sometimes I still have energy, but my children are tired." You go, CB—don't let those kids hold you back!

"How do you handle any interpersonal conflict that arises between you and your adult child when you travel together?"

When I asked Mom if she had any concerns about traveling with me, reminding her that I can be in a bad mood at times (particularly when I'm tired!), she replied, "Yes, you *do* get crabby. But I figure we can work through it, because we both love to travel together and see new things. That's what we did on our first trip together, and we've done it ever since." When I'm in a foul mood, Mom's strategy for handling me without making my mood (or the situation) worse is to avoid addressing concerns "in the heat of the moment." When things have calmed down a bit (perhaps as we're having a cocktail), she'll ask if I'm having an issue with her or if there's something else going on that she can help me resolve. Her "let me help" approach reminds me that there's not much we can't figure out together—a team mentality that usually helps us laugh about the situation (and my overreaction).

Mom offers two additional recommendations for avoiding conflict when aging parents and their adult children travel together:

- "Have some time to yourself, even if it's just 30 minutes or so a day. That little bit of space will do wonders—particularly if the other person is starting to get on your nerves."

- "Get a room with a separate seating area. Even if you don't spend much time in the room, being on top of each other in a small space can cause tension even in the best of relationships. If possible, book a room with enough breathing room for everyone."

Like Mom, most of the survey respondents consider communication the best tool for handling interpersonal conflict, with more than half of them saying they "talk it out" if a problem occurs or if they and their children are getting irritated with one another. Many also recognize the value of taking a break in order to calm down. "Take time outs!" urged Sally (72) from Indiana. Sylvia (57) from Rhode Island offered a similar recommendation: "If [my son] gets me mad, I still tell him off and then take a time out—away from him!" Clearly, travelers of all ages can benefit from a good old-fashioned time out! Respondents shared other thoughts on dealing with interpersonal conflict during trips with their children:

- "I stay firm on what I feel is best, but try very hard to make a conflict [into] a compromise." *(Mary Louisa, 55, Florida)*

- "I'm the parent! They wouldn't dare argue!" *(Robin, 58, Illinois)*

- "Change the subject." *(Diane, 70, New Jersey)*

- "I just keep my mouth shut. And let them do what they want." *(Frances, 83, Louisiana)*

- "Never argue." *(Oralia, 61, Texas)*

- "Give them space." *(Debbie, 55, Michigan)*

- "Love, patience, and respect." *(Reta, 60, Alabama)*

- "Same way I always have: I bite my tongue—a little more since they grew up." *(Ann, 62, South Carolina)*

- "I ignore her." *(Edna, 64, North Carolina)*

Many respondents mentioned one particular area of potential conflict: fear of being burdens to their adult children. Patricia (67) from Georgia wrote, "I don't like to feel like I slow [my children] down"—a sentiment shared by many aging parents. Early on in our travels together, I learned that if Mom thought I felt hassled by having her on vacation with me, that feeling would destroy any chance she had of having fun. So when we travel together, I make it a point to reassure her (through both words and actions) that she's not a burden to me. Communication is key: if you're worried that your adult children perceive you as an inconvenient annoyance, speak with them about this in a quiet moment. Explain how you're feeling and ask what you can do to make things easier for them. Taking the time to "talk it out" and make adjustments that help each other feel included and welcome can ensure that you all have a great time during your travels.

Nearly all (97%) of the survey respondents said that they love to travel with their adult children even though interpersonal conflict does arise from time to time. Mom says that when conflict arises, parents and children alike "should either talk it out or have a method for letting go and not engaging in the heat of battle," and I think she's absolutely right. Knowing that conflict is a possibility—and that *everyone* encounters it at some point—and having a plan for dealing with it will go a long way toward keeping tempers calm (and the trip a success) if it occurs while you and your child are traveling together.

"What suggestions do you have for seniors traveling by plane?"

"Drink water" said most of the survey respondents. That's great advice for anyone but especially wise counsel for seniors, because people can become dehydrated more quickly as they age. I was surprised to see that the second most popular recommendation was to bring slippers to wear on the plane—a suggestion that doesn't work so well for Mom, whose feet swell: if she took her shoes off on a plane, I'm not sure she could get them back on when we arrived at our destination. (If you decide to put on slippers during your flight, make sure that your regular shoes aren't too tight, in case your feet swell.) Here are some additional recommendations for seniors traveling by plane:

- "Allow yourself extra time. It's better to spend three hours waiting in an airport than to miss your plane because you didn't have enough time to get from one end of the terminal to the other." *(Sandra, 64, Alabama)*
- "Get an aisle seat." *(Jodie, 75, Arizona)*
- "Call ahead if you need special services." *(Deborah, 64, Georgia)*

- "Boost your immune system by eating right and taking some extra vitamin C prior to and during the flight." *(Alicia, 62, Florida)*

- "Pay a little extra for the most convenient flight (direct flights or shorter layovers)." *(Debbie, 55, Michigan)*

- "Wear comfortable things." *(Diane, 70, New Jersey)*

- "Don't take too much luggage. Take only what you need." *(Frances, 83, Louisiana)*

- "Never travel by plane!" *(Manuel, 59, Texas)*

"What suggestions do you have for seniors traveling by car?"

Many of the survey respondents have taken many trips by car and had some great recommendations based on their experiences. The predominant recommendations were "stop often to stretch your legs" and "plan on frequent bathroom breaks." Here's some more useful advice:

- "Bring a good book and a sense of humor. I sit in the back so I don't critique the driving." *(Barbara, 83, Massachusetts)*

- "Another driver to share duties, and OnStar or something similar." *(Sally, 72, Indiana)*

- "Be sure to travel in a vehicle that gives you room to be comfortable." *(Patricia, 67, Georgia)*

- "Napping is good." *(CB, 66, Oregon)*

- "Don't drive sleepy or tired." *(Alicia, 62, Florida)*

- "Plenty of pillows." *(Reta, 60, Alabama)*

- "Travel by plane." *(Diana, 57, California)*

- "[Buy services from] AAA." *(Janet, 69, Texas)*

- "Pick an audiobook and listen to it." *(Myrna, 73, Florida)*

"Do you have any other advice or comments that you'd like to share?"

The survey respondents had plenty of general travel advice to offer, too. In this list you're certain to find something that can help you plan and execute your own trip with your adult child!

- "Plan a short trip to start to see how it goes. Do something you all enjoy in common." *(Oralia, 61, Texas)*

- "Try to keep up with your meds. Try not to get off schedule." *(Manuel, 59, Texas)*

- "A positive attitude is key to travel." *(Mary Louisa, 55, Florida)*

- "Give each other lots of space." *(Jodie, 75, Arizona)*

- "Let them plan what they want, and [you can] stay in the room if you're tired." *(Marjean, 77, Texas)*

- "Have a flexible schedule, because it will allow you to be more relaxed." *(Sandra, 64, Alabama)*

- "Be realistic and honest about each person's abilities and limitations, and consider these when planning your trip. Share these with your travel agent as well, so that he or she can advise you on activities that match [everyone's] skills and interests." *(Sharon, 58, Texas)*

- "A cruise is a great way to travel with family. There are multiple things to do daily, and you can spend some or all of the day and night together—but only as much as you want." *(Nancy, 55, Florida)*

- "Traveling with three generations is fun, but get teenagers their own room!" *(Sally, 72, Indiana)*

"What would you say to a senior who is undecided about traveling with his or her adult child?"

The vast majority of respondents expressed the same sentiment: "Do it!" Most felt it was worth taking a chance on a trip together and risking the uncertainties and challenges of travel, if it meant being able to get to know their children on a deeper level and as adults. Here are even more words of encouragement—along with a few cautionary words of advice:

- "Go for it! Just be patient with them." *(Marjean, 77, Texas)*

- "Let them take care of you." *(CB, 66, Oregon)*

- "Do it while you can. It's a great chance to see things from your child's adult perspective and to be included in his or her life." *(Alicia, 62, Florida)*

- "Good, bad, or ugly—just do it. It's better than staying at home being a couch potato." *(Deborah, 64, Georgia)*

- "Pray a lot. Ask for wisdom." *(Jodie, 75, Arizona)*

- "If you have a wonderful child like mine, take trips every chance you get. Those are memories you and your adult child will treasure." *(Patricia, 67, Georgia)*

- "Try it for a weekend trip and see what happens. It's a great way to get to know [your child] as an adult!" *(Sally, 72, Indiana)*

- "Do it. It's a lot of fun! Keep an open mind." *(Frances, 83, Louisiana)*

- "It is a highly personal decision, but I love it. Everyone is different and has different likes and interests. Try to take that into account. Sometimes compromise is required." *(Sharon, 58, Texas)*

- "How well do you get along? If you argue a lot, it will be even worse. If you enjoy extended time together, go for it." *(Ann, 62, South Carolina)*

- "Study the dynamics of your relationship, because that should tell you if you get along well enough to travel together." *(Sandra, 64, Arizona)*

- "Make sure [your children] are mentally in a good place when traveling." *(Donna, 63, Texas)*

- "Try it—you might like it and learn a lot." *(Sandy, 74, Texas)*

- "Travel often and savor the time you get to spend with family." *(Sylvia, 57, Rhode Island)*

- "What are you waiting for?!" *(Diane, 70, New Jersey)*

Final Thoughts

With flight delays and the other myriad problems that can arise during a vacation, travel can sometimes be difficult. Whenever challenges appear, though, keep in mind the old adage "Be hard on the issue and soft on the people." In other words, work to resolve the problem, but always remember that you care about the people you're traveling with. Your travel-related issues will come and go, but your relationships with your loved ones will endure—and strengthening those ties is one of your main goals for traveling together.

Whether or not you encounter any logistical problems during your travels, any trip you take with your adult children will still always give you an opportunity to connect with each other. Spending vacation time together can strengthen your relationship—sometimes in new and unexpected ways. So seize these opportunities when they come your way. Stacy (58) from Washington nailed it on the head in her comments about traveling with adult children:

> As parents, we spent a great deal of time and effort teaching our kids while they were growing up. Let them teach you when you travel together. And when you feel frustrated or tired, ask yourself, "What's the worst thing that could happen right

now?" You may realize that what you thought was a big deal actually isn't. Be willing to be flexible and in the moment.

· · · · ·

This book grew out of my own travels around the world with my mom. Through our many journeys and many miles together, I've learned so much about her—and about myself, too. But the benefits of travel go both ways, and Mom will be the first to say that she's learned a lot as well. And with that in mind, I'll let her have the final word here:

> I didn't really understand how well I did in raising my children until I traveled with them. They all live in different states now, so I don't share much of their day-to-day lives. But when I see how well they plan and coordinate our trips together—and then pull them off—I realize that I did a pretty good job with them. Through travel, I really get to see how my kids have grown into capable adults, and I'm so happy to be able to connect with them this way!

APPENDIX 1

RESOURCES

This section includes helpful resources, organized by chapter. Although I have firsthand experience with some of the companies and websites listed here, I am familiar with most only through secondhand recommendations from friends, travel professionals, and travel-related websites and forums. Therefore, inclusion of any organization or resource here does not imply endorsement. Also keep in mind that although the contact information provided here is current as of this writing, it may have changed by the time you read this book. (If you find a URL or phone number that no longer works, an Internet search for that organization's name will likely lead you to updated information.)

I encourage you to use these lists as a starting point for your own research and (as with any consumer endeavor) to investigate all products, services, and claims thoroughly.

Chapter 1

· · · · · · · · · · · ·

- **Sydney Opera House Access Tour (limited mobility):**
www.sydneyoperahouse.com/Visit/Accessibility_Mobility.aspx,
tourism@sydneyoperahouse.com, +61 2 9250 7250

- **Sydney Harbour Bridge Climb:** www.bridgeclimb.com,
admin@bridgeclimb.com, +61 2 8274 7777

Chapter 2

· · · · · · · · · · · ·

- **Road Scholar:** www.roadscholar.org, registration@roadscholar.org,
+1 800 454 5768

Volunteer travel programs

- **Cross-Cultural Solutions:** www.crossculturalsolutions.org,
info@crossculturalsolutions.org, +1 914 632 0022

- **American Archaeology Abroad:** www.americanarchaeology
abroad.org, AarchaeologyA@gmail.com, +1 814 876 2780

- **Earthwatch Institute (U.S. office):** www.earthwatch.org,
info@earthwatch.org, +1 800 776 0188 or +1 978 461 0081
(visit the website for contact info for offices outside the U.S.)

- **Global Citizens Network:** www.globalcitizens.org, info@global
citizens.org, +1 800 892 0022 or +1 612 436 8270,
fax +1 612 436 8298

- **Global Service Corps:** www.globalservicecorps.org,
gsc@globalservicecorps.org, +1 503 954 1659

- **Global Volunteers:** www.globalvolunteers.org, email@global
volunteers.org, +1 800 487 1074, fax +1 651 482 0915

- **Globe Aware:** www.globeaware.org, info@globeaware.com,
+1 877 588 4562, fax +1 214 824 4563

- ○ **Habitat for Humanity International (headquarters and U.S. office):** www.habitat.org, info@habitat.org, + 1 800 HABITAT or +1 229 924 6935 *(visit the website for contact info for offices outside the U.S.)*

- ○ **Lead Adventures:** www.lead-adventures.com, info@lead-adventures.com, +1 800 579 3905 or +1 593 2254 1633

- ○ **Oceanic Society Expeditions:** www.oceanic-society.org, +1 800 326 7491 or +1 415 256 9604, fax +1 415 256 9434

- • **Centers for Disease Control and Prevention-traveler's health:** wwwnc.cdc.gov/travel, +1 800 CDC INFO, TTY +1 888 232 6348

Beach/amphibious wheelchair rentals

- ○ **Citizens' Right to Access Beaches (New Jersey):** www.crabnj.com, +1 732 361 2722

- ○ **De-Bug Wheelchairs (list of rental vendors in the coastal regions in the U.S. and the U.K.):** www.beachwheelchair.com/rentals.htm, kmdeming@aol.com, +1 850 478 5765, fax +1 850 476 3361

- ○ **ForHandicapTravelers.com (Mexican Caribbean):** www.forhandicaptravelers.com/amphibious-chair.htm, + 52 998 251 5385

- • **Information and Technical Assistance on the Americans with Disabilities Act:** www.ada.gov, +1 800 514 0301, TTY +1 800 514 0383

Wheelchair rentals

- ○ **Scootaround (North America):** www.scootaround.com, info@scootaround.com, + 1 888 441 7575 or +1 204 982 0657, fax +1 204 478 1172

- **Care Vacations (cruise ships):** www.carevacations.com, csa@carevacations.com, +1 877 478 7827 or +1 780 986 6404, fax +1 800 648 1116

- **Special Needs Group / Special Needs at Sea (cruise ships and worldwide destinations):** www.specialneedsatsea.com, + 1 800 513 4515 or +1 954 585 0575, fax +1 800 513 4516 or +1 954 585 0577

- **CARE Medical Equipment (Florida):** www.caremedical equipment.com, +1 800 741 2282 or +1 407 856 2273

Wheelchair-accessible van rentals

- **Wheelchair Getaways (U.S. and Canada):** www.wheelchair getaways.com, info@wheelchairgetaways.com, +1 800 536 5518 or +1 425 353 8213, fax +1 425 355 6159

- **Wheelchair Travel (U.K.):** www.wheelchair-travel.co.uk, trevor@wheelchair-travel.co.uk, +44 1483 237 688, fax +44 0 1483 237 772

- **DisabledTravelers.com (list of rental vendors throughout the world):** www.disabledtravelers.com/accessible_van_rentals.htm, jeremy@disabledtravelers.com

- **Wheelers Mobility (Arizona):** www.wheelersvanrentals.com

- **Mobility International USA's tips for choosing a wheelchair to take on travel outside the U.S.:** www.miusa.org/resource /tipsheet/choosingchairs

Chapter 3

. . . .

- **Douglas Zeiger, M.D. (travel medicine specialist):**
  www.travelmedicinenyc.com, +1 212 725 0580

- **Transportation Security Administration airport security screening
  rules and regulations:** www.tsa.gov/traveler-information,
  TSA-contactcenter@tsa.dhs.gov, +1 866 289 9673

- **U.S. Department of Transportation regulations for
  accommodating disabilities (including allowances for portable
  oxygen concentrators) on board airplanes:**
  www.dot.gov/airconsumer/disability, +1 202 366 4000

- **Federal Aviation Administration requirements for allowing
  portable oxygen concentrators on board airplanes:**
  www.faa.gov/about/initiatives/hazmat_safety, +1 866 TELL FAA

- **Airline Oxygen Council of America:**
  www.airlineoxygencouncil.org, jcollins@alpha-1foundation.org

- **National Home Oxygen Patients Association:**
  www.homeoxygen.org, execoffice@homeoxygen.org,
  +1 888 NHOPA 44

- **Sydney Opera House event tickets:** www.sydneyoperahouse.com,
  bookings@sydneyoperahouse.com, +61 2 9250 7777

- **WineSkin (transport bag for breakable items such as wine
  bottles):** www.wineskin.net

- **Transportation Security Administration regulations on
  transporting alcohol:** www.tsa.gov/traveler-information/alcoholic
  -beverages, TSA-contactcenter@tsa.dhs.gov, +1 866 289 9673

- **U.S. Customs and Border Protection regulations on bringing
  alcohol into the U.S.:** help.cbp.gov/app/answers/detail/a_id/190/~
  /bringing-alcohol-(including-homemade-wine)-to-the-u.s.-for
  -personal-use, +1 877 227 5511, TDD +1 866 880 6582

Chapter 4

. . . .

- **Douglas Zeiger, M.D., travel medicine specialist:**
  www.travelmedicinenyc.com, +1 212 725 0580

- **Centers for Disease Control and Prevention destination-specific
  travel recommendations:** wwwnc.cdc.gov/travel/destinations/list,
  +1 800 CDC INFO, TTY +1 888 232 6348

- **NHS National Services Scotland website for information on
  travel vaccines and diseases in other countries (recommended
  by travel medicine specialist Douglas Zeiger):**
  www.fitfortravel.nhs.uk

Lists of physicians and hospitals throughout the world

- ○ **U.S. Department of State website on finding a doctor or
  embassy abroad:** www.usembassy.gov (click on the name of the
  country you're visiting, then select "U.S. Citizen Services")

- ○ **Patients Beyond Borders:** www.patientsbeyondborders.com,
  +1 919 924 0636

- ○ **Medeguide:** www.medeguide.com, +66 2762 7851,
  fax +1 66 2762 7852

- **Social Security coverage outside the U.S.:**
  www.ssa.gov/international, +1 800 772 1213, TTY +1 800 325 0778

- **Medicare coverage outside the U.S.:** www.medicare.gov/coverage
  /travel-need-health-care-outside-us.html, +1 800 MEDICARE,
  TTY +1 877 486 2048

- **Medigap coverage outside the U.S.:** www.medicare.gov
  /supplement-other-insurance/medigap/whats-medigap.html

- **Combs & Company (full-service insurance brokerage firm):** www.combsandco.com, info@combsandco.com, +1 646 736 3737, fax +1 646 365 4564

- **InsureMyTrip (travel insurance aggregator):** www.insuremy trip.com, customercare@insuremytrip.com, +1 800 487 4722 or +1 401 773 9300, fax +1 401 921 4530

Chapter 5

. . . .

- **Better Business Bureau:** www.bbb.org, + 1 703 276 0100

- **United States Tour Operators Association:** www.ustoa.com, information@ustoa.com, +1 212 599 6599, fax +1 212 599 6744

- **National Tour Association:** www.ntaonline.com, +1 800 682 8886 or +1 859 264 6450, fax +1 859 264 6570

- **American Society of Travel Agents:** www.asta.org, askasta@asta.org, +1 800 ASK ASTA or +1 703 739 2782

- **TripAdvisor:** www.tripadvisor.com, +1 617 670 6300, fax +1 617 670 6301

- **Virtualtourist:** www.virtualtourist.com, feedback@virtual tourist.com

- **USPS hold-mail service:** holdmail.usps.com/holdmail, +1 800 ASK USPS, TDD/TTY call +1 800 877 8339 and ask for +1 800 275 8777

- **Suggested packing checklists:** (see appendix 2)

- **Transportation Security Administration regulations for traveling with medically necessary liquids, gels, and aerosols:** www.tsa.gov/traveler-information/medically-necessary -liquids-gels-and-aerosols, TSA-ContactCenter@tsa.dhs.gov, +1 866 289 9673

- **Transportation Security Administration information for travelers with disabilities and medical conditions:** www.tsa.gov/traveler-information/travelers-disabilities-and-medical-conditions, TSA-contactcenter@tsa.dhs.gov, +1 866 289 9673

- **U.S. Department of Transportation regulations for accommodating disabilities (including allowances for portable oxygen concentrators) on board airplanes:** www.dot.gov/airconsumer/disability, +1 202 366 4000

- **Federal Aviation Administration requirements for allowing portable oxygen concentrators on board airplanes:** www.faa.gov/about/initiatives/hazmat_safety, +1 866 TELL FAA

- **Airline Oxygen Council of America:** www.airlineoxygencouncil.org, jcollins@alpha-1foundation.org

- **National Home Oxygen Patients Association:** www.homeoxygen.org, execoffice@homeoxygen.org, +1 888 NHOPA 44

Chapter 7
. . . .

- **Airfarewatchdog (for monitoring airfare price fluctuations):** www.airfarewatchdog.com, questions@airfarewatchdog.com

- **Transportation Security Administration homepage:** www.tsa.gov, TSA-contactcenter@tsa.dhs.gov, +1 866 289 9673

- **Transportation Security Administration rules for older travelers:** www.tsa.gov/traveler-information/screening-passengers-75-and-older, TSA-contactcenter@tsa.dhs.gov, +1 866 289 9673

- **TSA PreCheck Program:** www.tsa.gov/tsa-precheck-application-program, TSA-contactcenter@tsa.dhs.gov, +1 866 289 9673

- **Transportation Security Administration regulations for traveling with medically necessary liquids, gels, and aerosols:** www.tsa.gov/traveler-information/medically-necessary-liquids-gels -and-aerosols, TSA-contactcenter@tsa.dhs.gov, +1 866 289 9673

- **Transportation Security Administration information for travelers with disabilities and medical conditions:** www.tsa.gov/traveler-information/travelers-disabilities-and-medical -conditions, TSA-contactcenter@tsa.dhs.gov, +1 866 289 9673

- **U.S. Department of Transportation regulations for accommodating disabilities (including allowances for portable oxygen concentrators) on board airplanes:** www.dot.gov/airconsumer/disability, +1 202 366 4000

Chapter 8

. . . .

- **Two-player card games**

  - en.wikipedia.org/wiki/Category:Two-player_card_games

  - www.pagat.com/number/2_players.html

  - www.thedatingdivas.com/just-the-two-of-us/50-card-games-for -2-people

- **Jenga (wooden block game):** www.jenga.com

Security bags, money belts, and body wallets for travel

  - **Pacsafe:** www.pacsafe.com/travel-accessories-wallets/body -wallets-money-belts.html, ussupport@pacsafe.com, +1 206 722 7233, fax +1 877 306 1181

  - **Travelsmith:** www.travelsmith.com/travel-accessories /security-bags-belts-wallets, service@travelsmith.com, +1 800 770 3387, fax +1 800 950 1656

○ **Rick Steves:** travelstore.ricksteves.com/catalog/index.cfm
?fuseaction=catalog&parent_id=124, rick@ricksteves.com,
+1 425 771 8303, fax +1 425 771 0833

Chapter 9
. . . .

- **U.S. embassies and consulates:** www.usembassy.gov

- **Social Security coverage outside the U.S.:** www.ssa.gov
/international, +1 800 772 1213, TTY +1 800 325 0778

- **Medicare coverage outside the U.S.:** www.medicare.gov/coverage
/travel-need-health-care-outside-us.html, +1 800 MEDICARE,
TTY +1 877 486 2048

- **Medigap coverage outside the U.S.:** www.medicare.gov
/supplement-other-insurance/medigap/whats-medigap.html

- **Combs & Company (full-service insurance brokerage
firm):** www.combsandco.com, info@combsandco.com,
+1 646 736 3737, fax +1 646 365 4564

- **InsureMyTrip (travel insurance aggregator):** www.insuremytrip
.com, customercare@insuremytrip.com, +1 800 487 4722 or
+1 401 773 9300, fax +1 401 921 4530

- **Centers for Disease Control and Prevention-traveler's health:**
wwwnc.cdc.gov/travel, +1 800 CDC INFO,
TTY +1 888 232 6348

- **Centers for Disease Control and Prevention destination-specific
travel recommendations:** wwwnc.cdc.gov/travel/destinations/list,
+1 800 CDC INFO, TTY +1 888 232 6348

- **Assisted Vacation (nursing staff to accompany clients on their vacations):** www.assistedvacation.com, thomas@assistedvacation.com, +1 828 273 4323

- **Transportation Security Administration regulations for traveling with medically necessary liquids, gels, and aerosols:** www.tsa.gov/traveler-information/medically-necessary-liquids-gels-and-aerosols, TSA-contactcenter@tsa.dhs.gov, +1 866 289 9673

- **Transportation Security Administration information for travelers with disabilities and medical conditions:** www.tsa.gov/traveler-information/travelers-disabilities-and-medical-conditions, TSA-contactcenter@tsa.dhs.gov, +1 866 289 9673

- **U.S. Department of Transportation regulations for accommodating disabilities (including allowances for portable oxygen concentrators) on board airplanes:** www.dot.gov/airconsumer/disability, +1 202 366 4000

- **Federal Aviation Administration requirements for allowing portable oxygen concentrators on board airplanes:** www.faa.gov/about/initiatives/hazmat_safety, +1 866 TELL FAA

- **Airline Oxygen Council of America:** www.airlineoxygencouncil.org, jcollins@alpha-1foundation.org

- **National Home Oxygen Patients Association:** www.homeoxygen.org, execoffice@homeoxygen.org, +1 888 NHOPA 44

- **U.S. Chamber of Commerce:** www.uschamber.com, +1 800 638 6582 or +1 202 659 6000

- **AAA:** www.aaa.com, +1 407 444 7000

- **Alzheimer's Association advice for traveling with someone who has dementia:** www.alz.org/care/alzheimers-dementia -and-traveling.asp, info@alz.org, +1 800 272 3900, TDD +1 866 403 3073

Wearable GPS tracking devices and medical alert bracelets

- ○ **MedicAlert + Alzheimer's Association Safe Return:**
  www.alz.org/care/dementia-medic-alert-safe-return.asp,
  +1 888 572 8466, fax +1 800 863 3429

- ○ **Alzheimer's Association Comfort Zone:**
  www.alz.org/comfortzone, +1 877 259 4850

- ○ **Revolutionary Tracker:** www.revolutionarytracker.com,
  info@revolutionarytracker.com, +1 212 249 7807

- ○ **MedicAlert Foundation:** www.medicalert.org, +1 888 633 4298

- **National Kidney Foundation travel guide for kidney patients:**
  www.kidney.org/atoz/content/traveltip, nkfcares@kidney.org,
  +1 855 NKF CARES, fax +1 212 689 9261

- **Medicare Dialysis Facility Compare (information on dialysis
  centers throughout the U.S.):** www.medicare.gov
  /dialysisfacilitycompare, +1 800 MEDICARE, TTY +1 877 486 2048

- **Dialysis Finder (iOS app for finding dialysis centers in the
  U.S.):** itunes.apple.com/us/app/dialysis-finder/id478244404?mt=8

- **Dialysis at Sea Cruises:** www.dialysisatsea.com, info@dialysis
  atsea.com, +1 800 544 7604 or +1 813 775 4040,
  fax +1 727 372 7490

- **InsureMyTrip (travel insurance aggregator):** www.insuremy
  trip.com, customercare@insuremytrip.com, +1 800 487 4722 or
  +1 401 773 9300, fax +1 401 921 4530

Chapter 10

. . . .

- **Centers for Disease Control and Prevention-homepage:** www.cdc.gov, +1 800 CDC INFO, TTY +1 888 232 6348

- **U.S. Department of State travel information:** travel.state.gov, +1 888 407 4747

Online discussion forums for travelers

- ○ **TripAdvisor:** www.tripadvisor.com/ForumHome

- ○ **Lonely Planet:** www.lonelyplanet.com/thorntree

- ○ **Frommers:** www.frommers.com/community/forum-main

- ○ **Rick Steves:** www.ricksteves.com/travel-forum

- **Better Business Bureau:** www.bbb.org, + 1 703 276 0100

- **United States Tour Operators Association:** www.ustoa.com, information@ustoa.com, +1 212 599 6599, fax +1 212 599 6744

- **National Tour Association:** www.ntaonline.com, +1 800 682 8886 or +1 859 264 6450, fax +1 859 264 6570

- **American Society of Travel Agents:** www.asta.org, askasta@asta.org, +1 800 ASK ASTA or +1 703 739 2782

Travel insurance for lost or delayed baggage

- ○ **InsureMyTrip (travel insurance aggregator):** www.insuremy trip.com, customercare@insuremytrip.com, +1 800 487 4722 or +1 401 773 9300, fax +1 401 921 4530

- ○ **Travelex:** www.travelexinsurance.com/travel-insurance /baggage-insurance, info@travelex-insurance.com, +1 800 228 9792

- **Smart Traveler Enrollment Program:** step.state.gov/step, TTY castep@state.gov

- **U.S. Department of State website on finding embassies and consulates abroad:** www.usembassy.gov

- **Travelex (currency exchange):** www.travelex.com, retail.marketing@travelexamericas.com

- **Reviews of banking apps (iOS and Android):** www.magnify money.com/blog/banking-apps/#best-worst-mobile-banking -apps-100-banks-credit-unions

- **Reviews of credit cards with no foreign transaction fees:** www.nerdwallet.com/blog/top-credit-cards/no-foreign -transaction-fee-credit-card

Chapter 11

Photo-sharing websites

- **Photobucket:** www.photobucket.com

- **Flickr:** www.flickr.com

- **Yogile:** www.yogile.com

- **500px:** www.500px.com

Scrapbooking

- **Everything About Scrapbooking (information for beginners):** www.everything-about-scrapbooking.com

- **Scrapbook.com (supplies and ideas):** www.scrapbook.com

- **Pinterest (digital scrapbooking):** www.pinterest.com

- **Smilebox (digital scrapbooking):** www.smilebox.com/ digital-scrapbooking.html

Starting a blog

- ○ **The Blog Starter:** www.theblogstarter.com

- ○ **Blogging Basics 101:** www.bloggingbasics101.com/
  how-do-i-start-a-blog

- ○ **Blogger Getting Started Guide:** support.google.com/blogger/
  answer/1623800

- ○ **"Where to Start When Starting a Blog"** (*New York Times*):
  www.nytimes.com/2014/07/24/technology/personaltech
  /where-to-start-when-starting-a-blog.html

- **Spafinder:** www.spafinder.com

Chapter 12

. . . .

- **Transportation Security Administration information on traveling
  with children:** www.tsa.gov/traveler-information/traveling-children,
  TSA-contactcenter@tsa.dhs.gov, +1 866 289 9673

- **Federal Aviation Administration recommendations for child
  safety when flying:** www.faa.gov/passengers/fly_children,
  +1 866 TELL FAA

- **Flying with children (general recommendations):**
  flyingwithchildren.blogspot.com

- **U.S. Customs and Border Protection information about children
  traveling with one parent, with someone who is not a parent or
  legal guardian, or with a group:** http://help.cbp.gov/app/answers/
  detail/a_id/268, +1 877 227 5511 or +1 202 325 8000,
  TDD +1 866 880 6582

- **Transportation Security Administration homepage:**
  www.tsa.gov, TSA-contactcenter@tsa.dhs.gov, +1 866 289 9673

Organizations that offer senior travel discounts

- **AARP:** www.aarp.org/benefits-discounts/Travel-Benefits, member@aarp.org, +1 888 OUR AARP or +1 202 434 3525, TTY +1 877 434 7598

- **AAA:** travel.aaa.com, +1 407 444 7000

- **Expedia:** www.expedia.com, +1 800 397 3342

- **Travelocity:** www.travelocity.com, +1 888 872 8356

- **Sam's Club Travel:** travel.samsclub.com/sams/traveloffers/default.aspx, +1 855 680 6663

- **Groupon:** www.groupon.com/getaways, support@groupon.com, +1 888 375 5777

- **Entertainment:** www.entertainment.com, +1 888 231 SAVE

- **Amazon Local:** local.amazon.com, +1 866 395 2090

SAMPLE PACKING LISTS

In chapter 5, I discuss how to pack for a trip, including what medical supplies and clothing items to bring, and how to assist your parents from afar with their packing. To help them get organized (and who among us couldn't use a little more organization, right?), I recommend sending them a packing checklist well before your trip together.

Here are several lists I've created for different categories of items you might want to take on a trip. Don't bring *everything* you see here—few things are worse than overpacking (especially when you have to lug suitcases around!). Instead, use these lists to customize your own packing checklist with the items your parents will need during your travels.

(These lists also appear on the *Travel with Aging Parents* website at travel withagingparents.com.)

Note: If you want to bring liquids that are not medically required (e.g., shampoo, contact lens solution, lotion) in your carry-on bag, be sure to pack them in bottles that hold less than 3.4 ounces so you don't violate the TSA's regulations for these items. Liquids in larger amounts should be packed in your checked luggage. Medically required liquids in larger amounts can be brought in carry-on bags if you have the proper documentation for them.

ITEMS FOR ALL TRIPS

Medicines

. . . .

Prescription Drugs (provide this information for each one you bring)
Brand name:
Generic name:
Purpose:
Dosage amount:
Dosage frequency/schedule:
Prescription number:
Prescriber name:
Prescriber contact information:

Nonprescription Drugs (provide this information for each one you bring)
Brand name:
Generic name:
Purpose:
Dosage amount:
Dosage frequency/schedule:
Prescription number:
Prescriber name:
Prescriber contact information:

Medical Items (in carry-on luggage)

....

- ☐ Prescription drugs
- ☐ Complete information for each prescription drug (see template above)
- ☐ Doctor's authorization for each prescription drug
- ☐ Complete information for each nonprescription drug (see template above)
- ☐ Contact information for all doctors
- ☐ Sinus medication (spray or tablets)
- ☐ Airborne or vitamin C
- ☐ Hand sanitizer (gel or wipes)
- ☐ Sleep-aid medication
- ☐ Spare batteries for hearing aids
- ☐ Glasses case
- ☐ Spare pair of glasses
- ☐ Contact lens case
- ☐ Spare pair of contact lenses
- ☐ Contact lens solution
- ☐ Eye drops
- ☐ Compression socks
- ☐ Vitamins
- ☐ Epinephrine autoinjectors (with prescription)
- ☐ Portable oxygen concentrator (with prescription)
- ☐ Portable wheelchair
- ☐ First-aid kit:
    - ☐ Gas-relief tablets
    - ☐ Antacid tablets
    - ☐ Antidiarrheal tablets
    - ☐ Antihistamine tables (for allergies)
    - ☐ Candied ginger or other relief for motion sickness
    - ☐ Mild laxative tablets
    - ☐ Pain- and fever-relief tablets
    - ☐ Band-Aids
    - ☐ Topical antibiotic

Electronic Equipment (in carry-on luggage)

- ☐ Mobile phone and charger
- ☐ Laptop and charger
- ☐ E-reader and charger
- ☐ Tablet and charger
- ☐ Game console/player and charger
- ☐ Portable DVD player and charger
- ☐ Camera and spare batteries, charger, and spare memory cards
- ☐ Power cords, connection cables, and spare batteries
- ☐ Power converter/electrical socket adapters
- ☐ Earbuds (bring headphones instead for anyone who wears hearing aids)
- ☐ Small flashlight/reading light
- ☐ Magnifying glass

Paperwork (in carry-on luggage)

- ☐ Travel confirmations and reservations
- ☐ Itinerary
- ☐ Passport
- ☐ Driver's license
- ☐ Copies of all important documents (e.g., passport, driver's license, prescriptions, credit cards)
- ☐ Medical and vaccination records
- ☐ Insurance details (e.g., travel, medical, car, credit card)
- ☐ Information for embassies and consulates at your destination
- ☐ Information for local hospitals at your destination
- ☐ Information for hotels en route to your destination (e.g., at connection airports, in cities you'll pass through)
- ☐ Information for reporting lost or stolen credit cards
- ☐ Maps and directions

☐ Emergency contact information: people in your travel party

☐ Emergency contact information: people back home

☐ Addresses for postcards

Miscellaneous Items (in carry-on luggage)

☐ Cash

☐ ATM card

☐ Credit cards

☐ Debit card

☐ Traveler's checks

☐ Prepaid phone cards

☐ Guidebooks

☐ Foreign language phrasebooks

☐ Reading material (e.g., books, magazines)

☐ Entertainment options (e.g., playing cards, puzzles, games, music, movies)

☐ Travel journal

☐ Light jacket or blanket

☐ Water (after the security screening, either purchase bottled water or fill a reusable bottle)

☐ Snacks

☐ Fanny pack or money belt

☐ Sunglasses

☐ Photos of your luggage (for identification purposes if it is lost or delayed)

☐ Tissues

☐ Chewing gum or hard candies (to open your ear canal and relieve pressure)

☐ Eye mask

☐ WineSkin bottle transport bags

All-Weather Clothing (in checked luggage)

- ☐ Sturdy walking shoes
- ☐ Slacks/jeans
- ☐ Skirt
- ☐ Formal outfit(s)
- ☐ Formal shoes
- ☐ Jewelry and other accessories (e.g., scarves, ties)
- ☐ Socks
- ☐ Pajamas
- ☐ Robe
- ☐ Slippers
- ☐ Underwear (e.g., underpants, bras, undershirts)
- ☐ Lightweight windproof/waterproof jacket
- ☐ Sweater or fleece
- ☐ Umbrella
- ☐ Bag for day-trip excursions
- ☐ Corkscrew (note: do not put this in carry-on luggage)
- ☐ Workout clothes (including shoes)
- ☐ Swimsuit
- ☐ Swimsuit cover-up
- ☐ Belt
- ☐ Plastic bags for dirty laundry

Warm-Weather Clothing (in checked luggage)

- ☐ Shorts/capris/skirts
- ☐ Short-sleeved shirts/tank tops
- ☐ Sundress
- ☐ Sandals/flip-flops
- ☐ Wide-brimmed hat or other head covering
- ☐ Beach towel
- ☐ Raincoat/rain boots

Cold-Weather Clothing (in checked luggage)

- ☐ Coat
- ☐ Gloves or mittens
- ☐ Winter hat
- ☐ Scarf
- ☐ Winter boots
- ☐ Thermal underwear
- ☐ Turtleneck or crewneck sweaters
- ☐ Sweater or fleece (or light jacket suitable for indoors)

Toiletries (in checked luggage)

- ☐ Makeup and makeup remover
- ☐ Shampoo
- ☐ Conditioner
- ☐ Curling iron/straightener
- ☐ Brush or comb
- ☐ Hair styling aids (e.g., hairspray, gel, headbands, pins, clips, elastic ties)
- ☐ Deodorant
- ☐ Toothbrush
- ☐ Toothpaste
- ☐ Mouthwash
- ☐ Denture cream and cleaner
- ☐ Dental floss
- ☐ Facial cleansers
- ☐ Facial moisturizer/cream
- ☐ Nail-care supplies (e.g., clippers, file, polish, polish remover)
- ☐ Tweezers
- ☐ Cotton swabs and cotton balls
- ☐ Body lotion
- ☐ Shaving cream and razor
- ☐ Perfume

Toiletries (in checked luggage) continued . . .

- ☐ Personal hygiene products
- ☐ Shower cap
- ☐ Insect repellant
- ☐ Sunscreen
- ☐ Lip balm
- ☐ Birth control
- ☐ Travel-size laundry detergent
- ☐ Travel-size laundry stain remover

Items for Car Travel

- ☐ Antifreeze
- ☐ Jumper cables
- ☐ Motor oil
- ☐ Windshield wiper fluid
- ☐ Maps and driving directions
- ☐ Spare keys
- ☐ Pillows and blankets
- ☐ Ice scraper
- ☐ Small container of change for parking meters and toll roads
- ☐ Spare tire and tire iron

Appendix 3

SAMPLE ITINERARIES

Throughout this book, I've stressed the importance of including plenty of downtime in your travel schedule, keeping things at a pace that works well for everyone in your party, and taking your time to enjoy your vacation experience. If your goal is to work your way through all the "must-see" sites at your destination in as little time as possible, you may succeed in checking them off your list, but there's a good chance you won't remember much about them. And there's a good chance you'll exhaust your parents, yourself, and anyone else traveling with you.

To give you an idea of how to pace a vacation with an aging parent, I've included here portions of the schedules Mom and I have used on various trips. Along with the time and place information, I've included notes that offer further details or suggestions for some items. I hope that these sample schedules help you see how, with a bit of planning and a willingness to take it easy, you and your parent can enjoy a wonderful trip together!

Long Trips Overseas

Here are excerpts from the schedule for the trip Mom and I took to Australia in early 2013. My brother, his wife, and their twin daughters met us there (they were living in China at the time), so the planning had to account for both an aging parent *and* two toddlers!

Wednesday, January 30

....

2:20 p.m.   Depart Indianapolis. After plane changes in Atlanta and Los
               Angeles (each with a two- or three-hour layover—plenty of
               time to cover flight delays and getting to our next departure
               gate), we board our final flight to Sydney late in the evening.

               Several days before our departure, I contact Delta to con-
               firm wheelchair assistance (in which a staff member with a
               wheelchair meets us at the check-in counter and accompa-
               nies us to the gate) for Mom at all of the airports we're flying
               through. I also confirm that Mom and I have seats next to each
               other on all of our flights.

Friday, February 1

....

8:40 a.m.   Arrive in Sydney (yes, we are a bit grumpy after that long-
               haul flight!) and, after collecting our baggage and clearing
               customs, head straight to our hotel to rest until lunch.

               Several days before our departure, I confirm reservations
               for a car service to pick up Mom and me outside the customs
               screening area at the airport, and I obtain the driver's mobile
               phone number in case I need to reach him or her. I also contact
               the hotel to confirm our early check-in reservations (for which
               I've paid a half-day fee).

               When we arrive at the hotel, I confirm with the concierge
               that the hotel has arranged for us to rent a wheelchair for
               Mom's exclusive use during our entire stay.

1:00 p.m.   Three generations of Grubbs have lunch together at a
               restaurant next to the hotel.

               Not having to go on an expedition to find lunch lets everyone
               (of all ages!) rest and recover more from their long journeys.

5:00 p.m.   Private van pickup for sightseeing (2 hours), followed by a drop-off at Sky Tower for drinks and dinner.

The hotel concierge confirmed in advance that two child car seats were installed in the van before it picked us up.

9:00 p.m.   Private van pickup at Sky Tower for return to the hotel.

Saturday, February 2

11:30 a.m.   Private van pickup at the hotel for drop-off at the Sydney Harbour Cruise departure office for our cruise (3 hours).

In advance of this trip, we confirm with the cruise reservation supervisor that we will have two booster seats for the girls as well as a place to store Mom's wheelchair while we're on the cruise (because the boat itself is not wheelchair accessible, her wheelchair must stay ashore).

3:00 p.m.   Private van pickup at the Sydney Harbour Cruise office for drop-off at the hotel, where we rest until dinner.

Sunday, February 3

10:00 a.m.   Private van pickup at the hotel for drop-off at the Sydney Taronga Zoo for the Wild Australia Experience behind-the-scenes tour (2 hours).

In advance of this trip, we confirm with the zoo office our reservations for a wheelchair and strollers there.

5:15 p.m.   Val and her sister-in-law do the Sydney Harbour Bridge Climb (3 ½ hours) while Mom and the rest of the family hang out at the hotel and relax.

Monday, February 4

....

8:00 a.m.   Blue Mountains Tour director Sally Bray picks us up by van for our trip with Aussie Farmstay and Bush Adventures (10 hours).

I confirm in advance that the van will include car seats and have enough room for Mom's wheelchair.

Key Takeaways

. . . .

- In your schedule, include time to rest at the hotel after each activity. This is particularly important during your first few days at an international destination, when you're probably still recovering from jet lag.

- Also allow plenty of time for meals. Mealtime can sometimes double as rest time, which can be especially helpful on full days.

- On this trip, most of our activities involved sitting, which enabled Mom to have longer days without being exhausted. Also, riding in cars gave us all opportunities to take naps, though if we drove long distances we made sure to stop and stretch our legs every couple of hours.

- The Sydney Harbour Bridge Climb was beyond the abilities of both Mom and her granddaughters. So we worked out a way for some of us to do this while the others did something different. On trips involving people of varying interests and abilities, it's good to have options for activities they can do separately.

Short Car Trips

Good planning (with lots of downtime) can improve any vacation, regardless of its location or duration. Here are excerpts from the schedule for a long weekend trip Mom and I took together in 2011.

Thursday, July 15

....

9:00 a.m.   Depart Indianapolis by car for Chicago.

This drive usually takes only three hours. But Mom and I do it in five, which gives us plenty of time for a leisurely lunch and frequent stops whenever we need to stretch our legs.

2:00 p.m.   Arrive at hotel in Chicago and rest until dinner.

5:30 p.m.   Cab ride to dinner at a restaurant located as close to the theater as I can get (so we can walk next door rather than hunt down a cab).

Friday, July 16

....

8:00 a.m.   Breakfast at the hotel.

9:30 a.m.   Cab ride to Shedd Aquarium. As we visit the exhibits, Mom uses one of the aquarium's free wheelchairs. We have lunch here before taking a cab to our next stop.

2:00 p.m.   Arrive at the Art Institute of Chicago. Here, too, Mom uses a free wheelchair provided by the facility.

5:00 p.m.   Cab ride back to the hotel, followed by room service.

At the end of this big day, Mom is exhausted by the time we return to the hotel. So rather than go out for dinner, we decide to order room service and watch a movie while propping up our feet. It's a lovely ending to a lovely day!

Saturday, July 17

9:00 a.m.   Breakfast at the hotel, followed by a relaxing morning at
                 the hotel and lunch.

                 *After such a busy previous day, we take our time getting
                 started today so we are sure to be fully rested.*

1:00 p.m.   Cab ride to the Field Museum of Natural History.

                 *Mom uses one of the museum's free wheelchairs, and we
                 share a snack here.*

4:00 p.m.   Cab ride back to the hotel to rest before dinner and a show.

Key Takeaways

- During long car rides, be sure to stop every two hours or so to stretch
  your legs. These breaks can make a huge difference for anyone who
  has circulation issues.

- If you're going to dinner and a show, select a restaurant close to the
  show venue. Cabs can be scarce during prime times, and being within
  easy walking distance of the theater will enable you to get to the show
  on time.

- When driving to a big city, park your car at your hotel and use cabs to
  get around town. Navigating unfamiliar and crowded city streets and
  trying to find parking (especially when there isn't any next to your
  destination) can add unnecessary stress to your trip.

- If you're planning to visit museums or other attractions, contact them
  ahead of time to find their wheelchair-rental policies. If you can make
  a reservation, do so. If reservations aren't available (most places rent
  wheelchairs on a first-come, first-served basis), find out the best time
  to arrive to ensure that you get a wheelchair.

- Using a wheelchair and taking long meal breaks can help your parents have longer days out. During this particular trip, leisurely lunches and using a wheelchair enabled Mom to have enough energy to do multiple activities back to back.

- When planning a long and busy day, be sure to factor in time for meals and snacks, particularly if your parent is on medications that need to be taken with food.

INDEX

ABOUT THE AUTHOR

Valerie Grubb's father was a pilot, so she was born with travel in her blood. She began traveling solo at the tender age of four (when she wandered out of eyesight of her house one day), and since then she has continued to make exploring the world a priority while pursuing careers in both operations management and executive coaching. Val and her mom, Dorothy, took their first overseas vacation together when Dorothy was sixty-four, and in the more than twenty years since then, they have logged over 300,000 miles (and counting!). In response to the lack of available resources on the subject of seniors traveling with their adult children, Val began publishing *Travel with Aging Parents* (www.travelwithagingparents.com) in 2013, a blog that chronicles the triumphs (and challenges) of intergenerational travel with Val's signature "you can do this" flair. Val loves to hear others' travel adventures. She can be reached at vgrubb@gmail.com.

www.ingramcontent.com/pod-product-compliance
Lightning Source LLC
Chambersburg PA
CBHW021225130626
46554CB00004B/1368